D0525425

Chris Leonard has written for b
biographies and devotional works. She is the author of *Leaning Towards Easter*, *Waiting* and *Holding On and Letting Go*, all published by SPCK. This is her nineteenth published book. She enjoys leading creative-writing courses and holidays and often meets people who are inclined to believe that God exists, but who can't understand how a relationship with him would work – not for them, anyway. Chris loves drawing out the good that she sees in people and her writing and teaching spring from lifelong faith and a degree in English and theology. She is married with two grown-up children and lives in Surrey. Her website is at www.chris-leonard-writing.co.uk.

To all the people who were willing to share personal stories in this book of how their own relationship with God works. And to all those kind, creative, wonderful people in whom I see so much of God – yet who wouldn't say they know him at present. He knows and loves all of you!

IS GOD FOR REAL?

*Signposts and stories for
people who wonder*

Chris Leonard

First published in Great Britain in 2011

Society for Promoting Christian Knowledge
36 Causton Street
London SW1P 4ST
www.spckpublishing.co.uk

British Library Cataloguing-in-Publication Data
A catalogue record for this book is available from the British Library

ISBN 978-0-281-06205-8
eBook ISBN 978-0-281-06696-4

Typeset by Graphicraft Ltd, Hong Kong
First printed in Great Britain by MPG
Subsequently digitally printed in Great Britain

Produced on paper from sustainable forests

Contents

———◆◆◆———

Acknowledgements

I would like to thank all the people who checked the words of this book so patiently and especially the following for permission to include pieces of their own writing. Most have used real names: a few are disguised. Names are listed in order of appearance.

Beginnings

Patsy Cassidy, Tanya Neave, Vicky Larkin, Pauline Latter, Lewis Wallace, Rob Sutcliffe, Rob Cochrane, Irene Williams, Carol Close.

Relationship

Alex Mowbray, Roger Madge, Maureen Chapman, Hildegard Weinrich, Heiner Georgi, Jack Lu, Elizabeth Hudson, Ann Stringer.

Help

Anne Rasmussen, Rosie Berry, Ken Bryan, Roma Bell, Joan Mason-Martin, Robert Stephen, Martin Kruger, Gayle Scott.

Changing

Steve Elmes, Kathy Butler, Pauline, Cath Rathbone, Rachel Kamara, Jo Withers.

Communication, guidance

Veronica Heley, Rachel Kamara, Juliette Lambert, Annemarie Aurmoogum, Anne Reid, Jennifer Louis, Jo Withers, Wiebke Smith.

Questions, doubts

Alex Mowbray, Sandra Delemere, Bea Fishback, Hilary Langley, Elisabeth.

Outworking

Annemarie Aurmoogum, Paul Lambert, John Ripley, Hilary Allen, Fran Pyatt.

Introduction

'How can you relate with someone you can't see, touch or hear?' Carole asked.

My elderly mum, just out of hospital, had Carole to help her twice a week – a godsend of a 'carer'. Capable and loving, a 'people person' who does tremendous practical good, Carole had many urgent questions about Christianity. Mum, too weak to answer effectively at that stage, lent her one of my devotional books.

Carole devoured it overnight, then read it again more carefully before plying Mum with more questions. 'This sounds great, but how do you pray? Do you need special words?

'In the true stories in Chris's book, sometimes God tells people to do something, or "speaks" to them in some way. Do they hear an audible voice, or what?

'I've never been to church, you see, nor have any of my family. I don't know the Bible, nor any Christians, well. You say Christianity is about a relationship between God and human beings, but I'm struggling to understand how this relationship works out in practice.'

Mum phoned me. 'Can you find her another book? Not about whether God exists – Carole is inclined to believe that he does. Surely there's something, other than biographies about one person, which shows how relationships between God and human beings work?'

'There must be,' I said. After all, that's what Christianity is all about – relationship with God and how that affects our relationships with other people. I searched in vain for such a book. Then, one morning as I was waking up, God 'spoke' to me. Not with an audible voice but with an idea which fired 'ping' into my sleepy brain, dazzling as the moment of sunrise. My existing devotional books have true stories from a variety of 'ordinary' Christians alive today, plus some bits from the Bible, written two thousand or more years ago. If I wrote one for people like Carole, people on the edges of faith, wouldn't that format provide not proofs but great 'signposts'?

I could ask lots of different people how their relationship with God works out in practice, during crises sometimes but mainly in normal, everyday life. Together with bits from the Bible these would give a wide spectrum of examples – after all, no two relationships work exactly the same. I even had a title: 'Is God for Real?' Not 'Is God real?' – as in 'does he exist?' Plenty of learned and popular books discuss that one. But is he 'for real'? Can knowing him really be as life-changing, intimate and awesome as the Bible – and today's Christians – say?

I believe almost everyone, like Carole, has moments of glimpsing or sensing something way beyond this world – something eternal, transcendent, far bigger, more glorious, awesome or loving than anything else. We think, there really is more to life than we know – until 'normality' rushes in, strident for our attention.

An Old Testament word for 'salvation' means 'to create space'. I hope this book will allow you to do that – to pause a moment and reflect. I've divided it into bite-sized chunks; you might want to read just one of these a day.

So, is God for real? Is it possible for human beings to have a relationship with him, or is it all a big delusion? I'd like to thank all the people mentioned in the acknowledgements section who have let me share their stories here. All are true, though occasionally names have been changed. As you read their stories and the 'Bible bits' in this book I hope you'll feel more able to trust for yourself that such a relationship is feasible – and wonderful – and then 'prove' it in the only way possible, by entering into a relationship of your own with God.

Beginnings

To begin – to find our way into some new thing or relationship – can seem daunting. But, once we start, it may be easier than we think.

Here are some stories of people starting to understand that God is for real and beginning their relationship with him.

Seeing God as real in others

Patsy Cassidy writes:

> At seven years old I was enjoying a holiday in the mountains of Malaya with my mother and sister when one day everything changed. Japanese were invading from the north and no one had told us in our holiday bungalow that the whole hill station had been evacuated! When news did reach us, my mother called my sister and me to her. 'We're in great trouble and need God's help. Jesus made a promise that he would always be with us and especially so when two or three are gathered in his name. So now let's all three together ask him for his help.' After a simple prayer I remember thinking with relief: well, that's all right now – God is in charge!
>
> We had to flee with virtually nothing. The story of how we made the amazing journey to rejoin my father in Singapore is too long to tell here. Father worked as a banker and his job at that time was to organize the evacuation of civilian wives and children. He'd been very concerned when we'd failed to arrive from the mountains and was overjoyed to see us – but now he insisted, 'There's a ship sailing tonight and you mustn't miss it!' My mother was horrified, not wanting to leave him. However,

one of the few things she had rescued from the hill station was a book of daily Bible readings. It fell open at Micah 2.10, 'Arise and depart, for this is not your rest' (NKJV). She felt this was a message from God and knew she must obey.

The small ship, carrying rubber, was returning to its home port in Canada and her captain and officers had offered their cabins to women and children. We stood on the deck before departure. Japanese planes had started bombing Singapore and, to prevent the invaders taking the fuel, the Allies set fire to petrol tanks. It was against this vivid background that I watched my parents say their goodbyes without knowing if they would ever see each other again. Though not understanding the situation, I felt deeply distressed to see them in tears.

We set sail under cover of darkness, making for Ceylon, the ship zigzagging to avoid enemy submarines all the way. Our lifejackets had to be within constant reach and everyone on the boat was terrified – apart from our little family. My mother's faith helped her to stay calm and this had a great influence on both of us children. I once had a terrifying dream about a bomb. Mother came to the rescue, 'That was an abominable dream! Can you say the word "abominable" – "a bomb in a bull"?' Laughter released me from fear. I remember her making bath-times such fun as we used phosphorescent water from the sea – as well as some passengers' angry complaints at the happy laughter of myself and my sister. 'This voyage is no laughing matter but a very serious time!'

And then I had a remarkable dream. I was with Jesus in a wood. He was holding my hand as we walked beside a beautiful, clear stream. The surface sparkled and deep down I could see green weeds, flowing with the water. I felt totally safe and knew I was loved, absolutely. The wonder of this realization of Jesus' loving presence has stayed with me all through my life and been a help to me time and time again. I am still so grateful!

On disembarking at Cape Town, we found the South African people marvellously kind and hospitable to all of us refugees.

My family was invited to stay on a farm in the country where the lovely Christians prayed for my father, and many others, every day. My parents, deprived of any communication, did not know where, or how, each other were for years. In fact my father was interned by the Japanese and worked on the notorious Siam/ Burma railway in appalling conditions. He found us, still in South Africa, on his release. He had suffered greatly and, while he never completely recovered from his ordeal, we all recognized that God had indeed answered our prayers by reuniting our family. My mother's faith never wavered as she cared for him. I first knew that God was real from her.

Many people discover that God is for real through observing others who are close to him. I remember an advert for a breakfast cereal which showed children eating it, then setting out for school aglow with an orange 'cloud' of warmth and health. Well, life's not quite like that but I have often noticed a glow about those who live close to God. Their very faces reflect something of him, as well as their actions and reactions.

Patsy saw so many Christ-like qualities in her mother – courage, simple faith, fun and humour despite a difficult situation, peace, trust, endurance. And then she saw Jesus for herself, in a dream – the reality of which has stayed with her. Patsy wasn't young when I met her but had an energy, a glow, a life about her. Being with her made everyone feel better, more cheerful. She was good to be around. Not all Christians are – some allow only a very muddy reflection of God's love to show. That's not God's fault, it's theirs. But if you know any who radiate his love and goodness, try to spend time with them; ask them questions about their relationship with him. They'll probably point out their failings and say they're not very good Christians but you'll learn a lot from them.

These words from the Bible speak of the way human beings can reflect something of God:

I sought the LORD, and he answered me; he delivered me from all my fears. Those who look to him are radiant; their faces are never covered with shame. (Psalm 34.4–5)

We, who with unveiled faces all reflect the Lord's glory, are being transformed into his likeness with ever-increasing glory, which comes from the Lord, who is the Spirit. (2 Corinthians 3.18)

Who communicates about God?

In the beginning was the Word, and the Word was with God, and the Word was God.

He was with God in the beginning. Through him all things were made; without him nothing was made that has been made. In him was life, and that life was the light of men. The light shines in the darkness, but the darkness has not understood it . . .

The Word became flesh and made his dwelling among us. We have seen his glory, the glory of the One and Only, who came from the Father, full of grace and truth. (John 1.1–5, 14)

You've just read part of a beautiful New Testament poem from the start of the Gospel according to John. Despite its simple vocabulary, the poem is far from easy to understand. It is important, though, because it describes how God makes himself real to us.

John says he did that by sending his Son, who was also God, into this world as his 'Word'. This title 'Word' means many things but the most important is 'God-Communicator'. Jesus communicated with human beings about God not just through what he, Jesus, said or even what he did, but through who he, uniquely, was – God in human form walking this earth. In other words, if you want to see what God is like and experience his essence, look at Jesus. No other god has been born, lived and died here, fully human yet fully divine. No human being has

4

done, spoken and been exactly what God would do, speak and be on earth. These are quite some statements to ponder. No wonder John's few words seem deep!

Having mentioned titles and names of God, I'll say something here about a possible source of confusion. Christians use other names for God, like 'Lord' and 'Saviour' – as well as 'Father', 'Son' and Holy Spirit' – the three 'Persons' of the 'Trinity'. Exactly how three are one and one three remains a mystery – we'll never understand everything about almighty God! The important thing to grasp is that Father, Son and Holy Spirit existed together from the beginning and their relationship is a great model for all the relationships which I'm writing about in this book.

Christians also speak of the Bible as the 'word of God'. In the four Gospels, communication comes in a double dose as the Bible or 'word of God' tells stories about Jesus, the Word of God. So reading from these four accounts written of Jesus by Matthew, Mark, Luke and John is a good place to start if you're wondering whether or not God is really who he says he is. Most people find it easier to see a human being as real than they do a spirit.

Tanya Neave writes about how someone told her about the Word – both Jesus and the Bible – and of how that started her long and very real friendship with him.

A long time ago I was seriously ill, having developed several blood clots in my lungs after an operation. My family had been warned that I was likely to die. My marriage was breaking up, I was desperately worried for my three children and very frightened about what was happening to me.

It was then that I had an 'out-of-body' experience. I was somewhere on the ceiling looking down on my bed, surrounded by doctors. Then the ceiling opened. Shooting upwards through beautiful pink clouds I felt wonderful, free from pain and full of joy. I thought – if this is death, I will never be afraid of dying again. Some with similar experiences claim to have met with God, but I, a complete non-believer, had no such encounter. All I know is that I made a decision to come back for the sake of my children – and immediately was in bed, in pain, fighting for life once more.

So where was God in all this? I had no startling revelation nor any change in my circumstances. Today, however, I believe that he was there, giving me that choice to return and live my life as he had planned. He came to me in the shape of a night nurse who quietly placed Bible verses on everyone's bedside.

At the time I resented her taking advantage, as I saw it, of people confined to their beds. I threw my Bible verse in the bin. Then, feeling that I had been inordinately rude, after some minutes I struggled out of my bed, retrieved the verse and read it. The nurse, who had been watching all the time, came over and we talked half the night. I refuted everything she said, and she will never know how much she affected me that night, beginning a process that changed my life. I cannot remember the words she used, only her passion and her confidence in a God who was her friend, rather than some authority figure far removed from ordinary relationships.

I have since come to know that God for myself. My name is Tanya Neave, God's friend for 43 years.

The book of Acts and the letters which follow in the Bible also tell stories of Jesus, even though by this stage he's no longer walking this earth. Jesus met only a limited number of people during his 33-year stay on this planet – his physical body could be in only one place at a time. But now many people in many places can meet him, through those who follow him. Few respond as quickly as Tanya did – for most it's a much slower process. Nor do Christians follow Jesus, as he followed his Father, perfectly – far from it! Nevertheless, the reality of people's relationship with Father God through Jesus has been evident over the centuries, in all kinds of cultures, climates and circumstances.

Has anyone been a God-communicator to you, showing you Jesus, not so much by their words as by the quality of their evident friendship with him? Maybe the way it was done was less than perfect and irritated you – but don't let that stop you exploring further.

What's missing?

Do not be anxious about anything, but in everything, by prayer and petition, with thanksgiving, present your requests to God. And the peace of God, which transcends all understanding, will guard your hearts and your minds in Christ Jesus. Finally . . . whatever is true, whatever is noble, whatever is right, whatever is pure, whatever is lovely, whatever is admirable – if anything is excellent or praiseworthy – think about such things. Whatever you have learned or received or heard from me, or seen in me – put it into practice. And the God of peace will be with you.

(Philippians 4.6–9)

It's a mellow September afternoon with a cloudless blue sky. I'm sipping tea in my garden, under a pergola where black grapes are ripening. All's well with my world. But I don't assume this idyllic moment will last, even though I believe that God is real and loves me. Christians aren't promised a charmed life!

Anyone can understand the peace that I feel now. But God's peace which passes all understanding became real the other week to my friend Yvonne. Suddenly diagnosed with a malignant tumour on her kidney, she experienced utter peace before, during and recovering from the major operation which removed it. She told me that she'd felt cradled in prayer, safe in God's hands, even relaxed. She said, 'It's not like me at all, I'd have expected to be all anxious – but it's wonderful that I wasn't and I'm so grateful to God!'

It doesn't always work like that. When cancer threatened and I needed an operation, I was in a right state. And yet, despite my feelings, God brought me through. Of course feelings are important – key – in any relationship. But more important is faithfulness. With that we can survive hiccups in our emotions, whether in a human relationship or one with God.

Vicky Larkin writes:

At 23 years old I didn't believe God existed. Surely in this rational, scientific age, no one believed in anything supernatural? I attributed any dissatisfaction I felt to my circumstances. So for several years I had been living an '*If only*' life. It started with '*If only* I had a boyfriend, then I'd be happy!' The boyfriend came along; I was happy for a while. But, one after another, new '*If onlys*' followed. '*If only* we were engaged', '*If only* we were married', '*If only* we had our own home', and finally, '*If only* I had a baby'. Each time, with the fulfilment of the dream, came satisfaction; each time, the contentment proved fleeting.

Despite a loving husband, a beautiful baby and a home of our own, when I looked inside myself I saw restlessness and an aching void. Why? If something was missing, what? As I became more and more troubled, tensions arose in our marriage. Then, one afternoon while baby slept, I knelt by our bed and in desperation prayed, 'God, if you're there, help me.' Straight away, and to my total amazement, the room filled with peace – so real, so thick, I could have cut it with a knife.

I found God that day, and I've spent the next 40 years getting to know him better. He was not a bit like I imagined he might be, and he still surprises me sometimes. He has seen me through good times and bad times and has never let me down.

Jesus – and St Paul who wrote the words quoted above – would have read what we now know as the Old Testament of the Bible in Hebrew. The meaning of the Hebrew word *shalom*, usually translated 'peace', embraces 'wholeness', 'health' and 'well-being'. Vicky described something missing at the heart of her life. Some have called it a 'God-shaped hole'. When she became aware of this and asked God for help he didn't only become real to her, he filled her emptiness with his peace, *shalom*, wholeness.

Since that amazing moment at the start of Vicky's relationship with him she hasn't sailed along on an emotional 'high'. But God's been with her, in good times and bad, making up her lacks – as he did when I 'lost it' and spun into anxiety before my operation, instead of presenting my requests to him with thanksgiving and fixing my mind on good and lovely things.

In this relationship, God lives with us. That means he sees right through us, but he also sees us through. He completes us, inasmuch as we let him. We know he's real, because we know we were never whole without him.

Do you have a hole in your life? An empty place which needs filling? What if you asked the God of peace, of *shalom*, to fill it with himself?

Seeing . . . and believing?

'Which is easier: to say, "Your sins are forgiven," or to say, "Get up and walk"? But that you may know that the Son of Man has authority on earth to forgive sins . . .' [Jesus] said to the paralysed man, 'I tell you, get up, take your mat and go home.'

Immediately he stood up in front of them, took what he had been lying on and went home praising God. Everyone was amazed and gave praise to God . . . 'We have seen remarkable things today.' (Luke 5.23–26)

When Jesus walked this earth, often he chose to show people that he was who he said he was – God's Son – through miracles such as healing. People believed that he could work such miracles, crowding around him to such an extent that sometimes the really sick people, such as this paralysed man, couldn't come near. So lateral-thinking friends gate-crashed Jesus' teaching session by cutting a hole in the roof and letting the paralysed man down on a mat in front of the miracle-worker. I wonder what the crowd made of that?

But instead of healing him, Jesus surprised everyone by touching perhaps on the root of the man's particular problem – guilt. 'Declaring sins forgiven? Most irregular – the man hasn't even confessed any!' Religious leaders who were present became agitated. How dared Jesus? Only God could forgive sins! Well, yes, that was the point. Jesus' physical healings were but a sign of the more complete wholeness which comes when God forgives, removes guilt and enables people to start a relationship with him.

In effect, Jesus said to those who doubted him, 'Here's the sign that I really am God!' as the once-paralysed man picked up his mat and walked away. Not proof, but, as the crowd agreed, remarkable – Jesus' words and actions filled them with awe, which is only one stage short of worship. While their religious leaders remained blind, some 'ordinary people' were beginning to see something, to question – could this man, could Jesus, be God?

Pauline Latter, from Littlehampton, is a retired grandmother of four little girls and writes here of how she found God was for real – in both healing and forgiveness.

> In the 1960s, my two sons were born with haemophilia, an inherited condition whereby the blood doesn't clot properly. We were forever in and out of hospital. My nerves were torn to shreds. My marriage fell apart. Later, with a new and loving husband, I still used tranquilizers and sleeping pills to help me cope.

But one day, after speaking to a church minister about divine healing, an encounter with God changed my life. I'd gone to bed thinking a quick prayer might be the right thing to do. But even before I started, I felt as though in the presence of God himself and saw what I was really like against his purity. I'd never considered myself a 'sinner' but at Sunday school I'd heard about Jesus dying on the cross so that people's sins could be forgiven, so I asked God to forgive me and help in my turbulent life. The next morning I was walking on air and from then on didn't need my pills.

One day my youngest son, then about eight, developed a severe bleed into his stomach and was curled up in a ball in pain. As I prepared his treatment he said, 'Mum, shall I pray?' I'd forgotten to.

He called out, 'God, please take this b****y pain away!'

As I brought his treatment in, he jumped off the settee and walked upright to the table, pain-free – healed!

He said, 'Mum, is this a miracle?'

I thought perhaps it was!

Later, at around 14, my eldest son developed tonsillitis. Nothing new, except this time the doctor wouldn't prescribe antibiotics despite a big risk of his throat bleeding.

Next morning, at a Bible study group, we were reading about the power of Jesus raising Lazarus from the dead, when the phone rang. Steve said he was coughing and spitting up blood.

My friends prayed as I raced home on my bike. Steve's throat looked like it had been rubbed by coarse sandpaper – with white blobs bleeding furiously.

Steve was happy for me to pray. I said something like, 'The same power that enabled Jesus to raise Lazarus from the dead is in me because of the Holy Spirit and can heal Steve's throat.'

The bleeding stopped immediately, without treatment. When I looked again, his throat and tonsils were clear and the big swollen gland in his neck had gone down too.

So, Jesus still heals people today. Not always. I don't know why it happens at some times and not others. But maybe healings still act like signs for those who choose to see them – a bit like when I mislay my glasses and can't read things which are plain to others. That doesn't mean the printed words aren't real, nor that they are meaningless or untrue – my eyes simply don't focus as once they did. When people believed the earth was flat they simply couldn't 'see' that it was round; it seemed illogical – surely people at the other side of a globe would fall off? Silly examples, perhaps, but when it comes to God being real, some people will never see – and may well become all agitated and upset, as religious leaders did in Jesus' day. (You can read the moving story about Jesus raising his friend Lazarus from the dead in John's Gospel, chapter 11. That upset the 'religious' people too!)

Do you dare to allow yourself to draw closer, asking the Lord to help your eyes to see properly, so you can begin to glimpse more of who he is?

Words of life

As I've said, some people first glimpse that God is for real when they see the effect which knowing him has on another human being. Lewis Wallace writes:

My brother Jack was still a very young man when he contracted a disease that was to prove a 14-year death sentence. Not that he was aware of any such thing at the time. About to embark on a career in teaching, he hoped to marry his lovely girlfriend and had everything in the world to live for. At first he didn't worry about developing a limp. It wasn't until the local consultants were unable to diagnose the cause that he was seen by one of the top neurologists in the country and learnt that he had contracted syringomyelia. It would cause all the muscles of his arms and legs to waste away gradually, resulting in an early death.

His walking deteriorated until at last he had to be moved around the house in a wheelchair. He lost almost all use of his hands, so that I (as his very much younger brother) would sit at the living-room table typing out the letters he dictated to friends. Letters full of cheerfulness, with never a hint of what he must have been feeling inside.

It was clear that the end could not be far off when at last Jack couldn't even leave his bed. He had just enough strength in one finger to press an electric bell-push when he needed to be turned onto his other side. Then, one evening, as I was sitting with him, he asked me to read aloud a passage from the Bible: leaving me in no doubt that it was the one thing above all that had kept him going all those years. From Paul's letter to the Romans, chapter 8, I read out:

> Who shall separate us from the love of Christ? Shall trouble or hardship or persecution or famine or nakedness or sword . . . No, in all these things we are more than conquerors through him who loved us. For I am convinced that neither death nor life, neither angels nor demons, neither the present nor the future, nor any powers, neither height nor depth, nor anything in creation, will be able to separate us from the love of God that is in Christ Jesus our Lord.

Which is why I have always regarded that passage as the very words of life: words read at Jack's funeral, just as I wish them to be read at mine when that time comes.

No one can prove that Jack's extraordinary inner strength, peace and cheerfulness came from God, but they must have come from somewhere! Jesus often said only those with eyes to see will recognize the truth that is staring them in the face. I'm far from certain that anyone looking at me would see the difference knowing Jesus makes, in the way that Lewis did with his brother. Maybe Jack's suffering had stripped away all the trivial things of life, leaving only the bare essentials visible – as the harsh winds of winter strip a tree of its beautiful leaves, revealing its structure: the trunk and branches which support it.

St Paul, who wrote the words Lewis quoted above, also knew hardship. The following words are from his letter to an early Christian community and follow on from those quoted with Vicky's story. What do they tell you about the kind of God who lends a life such extraordinary structure and strength? Do you see this kind of thing in anyone you know?

> Whatever you have learned or received or heard from me, or seen in me – put it into practice. And the God of peace will be with you . . . I have learned to be content whatever the circumstances. I know what it is to be in need, and I know what it is to have plenty. I have learned the secret of being content in any and every situation, whether well fed or hungry, whether living in plenty or in want. I can do everything through him who gives me strength.   (Philippians 4.9–13)

Real in life and death

> 'Death is swallowed up in victory.' O death, where then your victory? Where then your sting? For sin – the sting that causes death – will all be gone; and the law, which reveals our sins, will no longer be our judge. How we thank God for all of this! It is he who makes us victorious through Jesus Christ our Lord! So, my dear brothers, since future victory is sure, be strong and steady, always abounding in the Lord's work, for you know that nothing you do for the Lord is ever wasted as it would be if there were no resurrection.   (1 Corinthians 15.54–58 TLB)

The day after her husband died, a friend's 3-year-old grandson sat on the stairs becoming more and more agitated. 'But where *is* Grandpa?' he asked, of anyone who passed. No one gave him a satisfactory answer.

Another friend's young son asked the same question as a coffin was carried into the crematorium's chapel.

'What's in that box?'

'Granddad's body,' she explained.

'Oh . . . Where's his head, then?'

Perhaps one reason why adults find death so hard to explain to small children is that, despite being one of life's few certainties, it remains a mystery beyond our full understanding or control. Sure, the body in the coffin isn't the real person, but what has become of his or her distinctive personality, memories, accumulated knowledge, humour, love? Hard to believe all of that is gone – exists only in our memories. Instinctively we sense that 'nothing [good] is ever wasted as it would be if there were no resurrection'.

Maybe that's why believers and non-believers alike invoke God at funerals. Faced with the dead body of someone we love, we need God and his promises to be real. So does the person who has just died!

Rob Sutcliffe, a Yorkshireman now living abroad, writes:

The brain tumour had taken its toll. Mum, always a fighter, couldn't fight this one. I'd paid a last visit, and was boarding a flight home, when finally she gave up.

We flew back a few days later for the funeral. I wouldn't have thought of going to 'view' the body, to 'view' Mum, had not my brother, influenced now by customs different from those I was used to, suggested it. But then I thought, why not?

The funeral director ushered my wife and me into a room lined with red velvet. There she lay, a pale, white figure in her open coffin – and at once I knew. This was just a shell, an empty case – even the face, especially the face, no longer hers.

Mum, already in another place, freed from pain and fear, was at home with her Lord. That's when I knew that there is life after death and a heaven, where our Father is waiting to welcome us home.

It's so good to know, before death, that Jesus is real and has prepared a home for us to go to. Jesus said to his followers before he died:

'Let not your heart be troubled. You are trusting God, now trust in me. There are many homes up there where my Father lives, and I am going to prepare them for your coming. When everything is ready, then I will come and get you, so that you can always be with me where I am. If this weren't so, I would tell you plainly. And you know where I am going and how to get there.'

'No, we don't,' Thomas said. 'We haven't any idea where you are going, so how can we know the way?'

Jesus told him, 'I am the Way – yes, and the Truth and the Life.'   (John 14.1–6, TLB)

Looking back, do you see?

In his heart a man plans his course, but the LORD determines his steps.   (Proverbs 16.9)

I've met many people who live like Christians but wouldn't call themselves that. Some go to church: others don't – but their lives are unselfish and cheerful; they do much good. Many are spiritually aware, believe that God exists, think Jesus was great and even pray. I can see Jesus in them but they say, 'No, I'm not a Christian, I don't have a faith.' I think they mean they haven't met Jesus for themselves, so they don't know him enough to trust him with their lives or to make him boss. But Jesus knows them and I reckon he's with them. He won't force anyone to have a relationship with him but he does guide people gently towards himself. As Shakespeare said, 'There's a divinity that shapes our ends, rough-hew them how we will.' Rob Cochrane, now in his nineties, writes of how that happened to him:

As a boy I was taken to church every Sunday by my parents. Then, during my teens, I grabbed the chance of learning to play the church organ, solely for pleasure I thought . . . until the organist left and I found myself appointed in his place.

My love of music matched by love of the stage, I spent many happy years with a major amateur company playing principal parts before becoming the producer. Happy in my married and working life, when one or other of my staff came to me with difficult personal problems, I would do my best to assist – feeling it was another part of my job. I've no idea how, with work pressures at their maximum, I found myself 'volunteered' into writing a weekly radio sketch for a Christian programme on a local BBC station – for seven whole years.

Disaster struck only well after retirement, when years of living through a trauma brought me to the verge of a mental and nervous breakdown. For the first time ever I kept finding myself praying the psalmist's words, 'Out of the depths I cry to you, O LORD' – with no apparent response. It seemed an eternity before the tiniest chink of light appeared at the end of the tunnel, and bit by tiny bit the situation improved. Then, though still vulnerable and uncertain, I began to realize how so many apparently independent factors had contributed to the solution. Too many to have been mere happenstance.

Even then it took a while before I could accept that God had indeed answered my prayers – but in his own time and way. Except that wasn't all. I began analysing what had motivated me in learning the skills which resulted in my still being a church organist: not to mention the far more complex skills that had enabled me to write dramatic radio sketches during what I now regarded as the most enjoyable time in my life. Had my 'independent' decisions all those years ago been influenced by the Holy Spirit all along?

In my new-found humility I questioned whether my present service to God wasn't wholly inadequate – until one Sunday, when I was playing for a service with such a small congregation that I was singing the hymns also. It required total concentration, yet a voice came from just behind my left shoulder: 'You *are* serving me!'

Totally shaken, I glanced around – to find, of course, that there was no one visible anywhere near me. Which was when I launched into a triumphant final verse of the hymn.

Most Christians are able to look back over their lives and tell any number of stories of how they can see now the way God was arranging things, even though it wasn't clear to them at the time. It's one of the ways by which I know he's for real! Events couldn't just have 'happened' like that. No human being could have planned them in that way, certainly not me! I say, 'Thank you, God, for the detail in which you work it all out.'

A different way

Irene Williams attended Sunday school as a child but, by her late teens, believed that God didn't exist and that Jesus was no more than a good man. She stopped going to church altogether.

Later, she and her husband decided that, just in case their daughter might want to join a church, they would have her baptized. Checking out a local church one Sunday, Irene couldn't find her way into the building and appreciated help from friendly Gillian – a late-arriving churchgoer who then sat with her during the service. Irene knew the words of the Anglican communion service but this was a modern version.

Why did some of the words appear to jump out of the page at her, as though highlighted, not in ink but in significance? For the first time ever she began to glimpse what it meant that Jesus died in order to forgive people.

Invited to the communion rail to receive a blessing, Irene felt what she could only describe as 'a presence' – and the curate's sermon seemed to be speaking directly to her, as though no one else were there. He spoke from Ephesians 2.1–10, about God's love and forgiveness and our need to 'die to sin'. I'm not a sinner, Irene thought! I haven't murdered anyone. Yet, still sensing that same strong 'presence' around her, she began to wonder if there was a God after all. If so, he seemed to be saying that his shoulders were big enough to take all she was carrying. But Irene wasn't aware of carrying anything heavy – her life was OK, she had no deep needs.

And then she started crying, weeping buckets – with no idea why. She felt surprised and a little hurt on noticing Gillian smiling broadly.

'It's OK,' said Gillian, 'I can see the Holy Spirit at work in you!'

Religious nut, thought Irene. At the end of the service the curate approached, also with a big grin on his face.

'Why are you so happy when I can't stop crying?'

He also said he could see God at work in her. 'Come to my office tomorrow and we'll talk about what is happening to you.'

To Irene's surprise, her tears began again the moment she entered his office. For 15 minutes she couldn't speak. The curate continued calmly with some paperwork. Then he told her, 'You have two choices – walk away and ignore God or ask Jesus to forgive you for not believing in him – and for all your sins.'

Irene thought, I can't walk away. I don't understand about my 'sins', but this is too powerful. I wasn't looking for God, so he must have been looking for me – therefore he must exist!

'I've never prayed out loud,' she said.

'Get on your knees and I'll pray. If you mean them, you say the words after me,' said the curate.

Irene did so, and felt as though hands were opening her up, making her clean and new inside.

'Read the Bible,' said the curate. She couldn't understand her old King James Version so she was given a *Good News Bible* in modern English and advised to read the New Testament plus some specific passages from the rest.

She did so for five minutes a day and saw some dramatic changes. Overnight she stopped swearing; her fear of spiders and of the dark disappeared. She could see now that she did sin. She'd always been critical of other people and would talk about them behind their backs – but now she realized how that hurt them and damaged relationships. Yes, she was a sinner – but now that she wanted to be different, God was helping her. Without knowing it, she had been carrying a big weight of guilt and of responsibility, but God's huge shoulders really could carry it all.

I asked Irene how, after all these years, she was different?

'I'm more patient, more caring and understanding, more tolerant and less demanding of people. I know God will show me if I do something wrong, often by giving me an uncomfortable feeling. Then it's not hard to ask for his forgiveness, for an opportunity to put things right, and that he'll help me to change and not do it again.'

Sin is wider than flagrant criminal behaviour – murder, theft, rape . . . It's rooted in the selfishness that's deep within all of us and causes most of the problems and pain, the guilt and shame in this world. It's a downwards spiral – ever noticed how guilt and shame propels you into hurting more people, or how the abused often become abusers themselves? But our self-centredness (sin) isn't an insoluble problem. God has provided a way out.

Jesus took on board all of the consequences of that downwards spiral in dying – as God, as a human being and as an innocent execution victim – in agony on the cross. Extraordinary grace, it reaches far beyond my understanding – but that is how God began to break the hold which sin and guilt have over us.

Jesus' resurrection gives us access to all the power we need to live differently. But first we need to acknowledge that his way is better than ours – and turn to follow him, let him be our 'Lord', our authority, 'boss' or mentor. That sounds cold but in reality it's the most loving relationship. If we put him rather than ourselves at the centre of our lives we will love whatever he loves – and he loves each one of us. He doesn't want us to change our whole personalities. He made us, and sees beyond all our wrong choices, bad habits and attitudes to all the good in us. He wants to help us to become the very best that we can be.

As we learn to love him with all our minds, hearts, souls and strength we will learn to love ourselves and our 'neighbours' (everyone else) equally. That's what Jesus taught, and if we could live our lives his way we would be free from selfishness and 'sin'. Most of us find that we mess up, often – but if we keep turning back to him and his ways he will help us to be motivated by love instead of criticism, jealousy, irritation, wanting our own way or whatever.

> God is so rich in mercy; he loved us so much that even though we were spiritually dead and doomed by our sins, he gave us back our lives again when he raised Christ from the dead – only by his undeserved favor have we ever been saved – and lifted us up from the grave into glory along with Christ . . . And now God can always point to us as examples of how very, very rich his kindness is, as shown in all he has done for us through Jesus Christ.

> Because of his kindness, you have been saved through trusting Christ. And even trusting is not of yourselves; it too is a gift from God. Salvation is not a reward for the good we have done, so none of us can take any credit for it. It is God himself who has made us what we are and given us new lives from Christ Jesus; and long ages ago he planned that we should spend these lives in helping others.　　　　　(Ephesians 2.4–10, TLB)

This passage, which so annoyed Irene at first, is quite a vision to live by, a real turn-around for anyone, including those considering themselves decent people who've never done any wrong. The Bible tells us to 'repent' of our sins. That means 'turn around and go the other way'. 'Doing it my way' won't work – it takes humility to grasp that. To stop being selfish and to start loving even unlovely others as he loves them, we need his help, his power. He'll set a pace which won't overwhelm us – we can ask him which attitudes, thought-patterns, priorities and actions he wants to help us to turn around right now.

If you want to begin a real working relationship with Jesus, here is the kind of thing you might pray: 'Lord Jesus, I want to put my trust in you and your perfect love. I have fallen so far short of that kind of love and goodness and have done my own thing rather than listening to you. I am sorry. I have hurt other people and hurt you. Thank you for dying on the cross so that I might be forgiven and have a new, clean start. Thank you that you accept me, love me and want me as part of your family. Please come into my life, Holy Spirit. Draw me closer and closer to you and fill me with your power to live my life your way.'

Endings and new beginnings

Carol Close is a single parent of three beautiful grown-up children and has spent most of her working life as a primary teacher in Lancashire. She writes:

I was 16 and angry when God exploded into my life.

That day I had travelled home from school, sneaking out at break. I wouldn't have cared if someone had caught me, but they didn't. A great sense of urgency called me home. Something was wrong.

The night before, I had argued with my father cruelly, knowing he was ill. Now it played on my mind and the nagging thought that had stayed with me all morning wouldn't let me go.

'There's something wrong,' it said. 'Run!'

I ran for a bus and got on. It slowed to a painful crawl.

'Hurry,' the voice said.

I got off the bus and ran. The voice inside my head kept on. 'Something is wrong . . . something is wrong.'

I opened the door to a house charged with an emptiness I couldn't explain. Routine took over and I found myself in the kitchen making tea. But like a haunting melody the emptiness wouldn't let me go . . .

'What if?' it said. 'What if . . . ?'

I sat with the food untouched in front of me. The sense of impending doom loomed larger.

I looked towards the empty hallway, expecting an answer. And then, like a flash of light imprinted in front of me, a picture formed before my eyes. Over in seconds, it was enough to send me reeling.

I saw two ambulance drivers in uniform struggling to carry a stretcher, my dad laid out between them. The picture disappeared and I was left with the inevitable. My dad was dead.

A vision, a picture, an image, a flash of life and death. The power of it flung me to my knees and I sobbed with great tears of grief and regret. 'I'm sorry,' I cried. A plea, a request, a 'Please forgive me for all the wrong things I've ever done to you. My father on earth. My father in heaven.' I cried, 'I'm so sorry.'

In that moment, a heaviness lifted from me and a great sense of freedom flooded my body.

That heaviness had weighed down upon me over the years. I got up, different, light, knowing that something had happened to me on the inside.

The door opened. My mum appeared, her face pinched and pale, stunned with shock, fighting back painful tears. The relatives followed.

'Your dad's dead, love,' she said.

I ran to her, something I'd not done for years. She was not normally the kind of mother you could run to.

'But I loved him,' I cried.

I didn't know what had happened to me. God living in me? Jesus dying for my sin? Jesus the man who walked on this earth, in heaven and able to heal and forgive me by the power of his Holy Spirit? Something was different.

I was different and my life was on a course with God. He was alive in me. My spirit had come alive with his. Suddenly, I knew him.

Anger returned as the days passed by. I kept noticing that everybody else seemed to have a father. My friends still had fathers. Even old people had fathers.

'Why have you taken mine, God?' I cried. 'Why my father? Why not someone else's?'

I was 16 and angry but now I had God to talk to and I knew that he loved me. He would take care of me.

'It's mine to give and mine to take away,' he said.

He was right. And I knew that he loved me, he would take care of me. He calmed my fears and held me in the darkest moments of each day. He had given me a new life, and it stretched out before me, full of hope.

Today, looking back 38 years, I cannot thank God enough for how he has helped me on my journey through life. In good times and bad God has stayed by my side, especially through hardship and pain. I have not always trusted, I have not always obeyed, but his amazing love has kept me through the years. I have changed along the way – just as well! I'm much nicer now than I used to be. God promises to make us more like Jesus in our character, and it was in the times where things seemed to be going wrong that I learned the greatest lessons about myself and others. I thank God for his ongoing forgiveness towards me, for his faithfulness and for his love.

Carol's story reminds me of three things. The first is of how one of my heroes of faith first met Jesus amid all the confusion and pain of the sudden death of his mother when he was a teenager. That traumatic, unlikely start has led not only to some great music and inspiring lyrics from U2. It's led to young Paul Hewson from the poor side of Dublin, now known as Bono, persuading rich and powerful world leaders, as well as 'ordinary' people, to give and work on behalf of the world's poor, marginalized and suffering, to further God's justice in this world.

The second is the words of another lyric-writer from several millennia ago:

> Let me hear joy and gladness; let the bones you have crushed rejoice. Hide your face from my sins and blot out all my iniquity. Create in me a pure heart, O God, and renew a steadfast spirit within me. Do not cast me from your presence or take your Holy Spirit from me. Restore to me the joy of your salvation and grant me a willing spirit, to sustain me.
>
> (Psalm 51.8–12)

We all need new beginnings – not just one, but many. Thank God that he never runs out or tires of these fresh starts for us.

The third is God's ultimate plan, which was never for hurtful arguments, guilt, sickness, pain, abandonment or death. Today he will redeem good from bad things which happen, bringing new life, new beginnings. But at the end of time there will be an ultimate new beginning. This is the ultimate hope of all who know, trust and follow him:

I heard a loud voice from the throne saying, 'Now the dwelling of God is with men, and he will live with them. They will be his people, and God himself will be with them and be their God. He will wipe every tear from their eyes. There will be no more death or mourning or crying or pain, for the old order of things has passed away.' He who was seated on the throne said, 'I am making everything new! . . . To him who is thirsty I will give to drink without cost from the spring of the water of life. He who overcomes will inherit all this, and I will be his God and he will be my son.' (Revelation 21.3–7)

Relationship

Have you ever thought about how you get to know someone? These days we all know a little about a lot of people we've never met. We can watch them on TV, read about or even Google for information on them. But only if we meet and spend time with a person, developing a close and trusting friendship, can we begin to say, 'I know that person well.' Think how different that is from simply knowing about someone – and how important real, live relationships are to us!

Thinking now about God – it's possible by various means to find out about and appreciate something of his work and character. But not until we get to know him for ourselves does a relationship form which becomes . . . what? Amazing, life-changing, central . . . I'm finding it even harder to put into words than describing what a close human relationship means to me. So forgive me for going all personal in the start of this section and drawing parallels with my closest human relationship – with my husband. I appreciate that many people aren't married, let alone happily, but hope that all who read this will be able to think of at least one close human relationship where love may not be romantic or perfect but is unconditional, mutual and real.

How do I know God loves me?

Maybe the question to ask is not 'Do I believe in God?' but 'Does God believe in me?' Knowing the track record of human beings, why would he believe in us, trusting us with his love? Yet he does.

How do we know that he accepts us as part of his family? Suppose I ask the same question about my husband. He said he loves me – still does sometimes. He shows me too – though no great romantic, he has even been known to bring me flowers! But love is more than words, a heady feeling or a dozen red roses. John shows he cares about me in all kinds of practical ways and shares his joys and concerns with me.

We've been committed to and trusting of each other through ups, downs and occasional flaming rows. Our 32 years of marriage have encompassed the birth and bringing up of children, various illnesses, joys, disappointments, joint projects, changes, risks, hard work – all sustained, ultimately, by our love and God's love. I can't prove that John, or God, loves me – but know that they do, through all I've experienced within those relationships. And others can sense that love too.

At one time I worked two mornings a week for the company where John is a senior software engineer and systems manager. He had his own office up the corridor: my base was in Reception. Both being busy, we didn't see much of each other at work. John's colleagues had known me slightly, for years, through various social 'dos' to which spouses were invited. All except Bob, a thoughtful American who had joined the company only a few days before I did. After about a month he spoke, carefully and quietly, to John. 'Say, where did we find Chris?'

'She's my wife.'

Bob's face relaxed. He smiled broadly. 'Gee, I *am* pleased to hear that. I thought you two were having an affair!'

It still makes me laugh – and wonder how Bob sensed something of that nature going on between us. We'd never kissed, cuddled or called each other 'darling' in the office. Love seems so intangible, so hard to put into words, and yet we know it's there – even in other people. It's the same with God's love. 'This is how we know what love is: Jesus Christ laid down his life for us' (1 John 3.16). 'We love because he first loved us' (1 John 4.19).

You might want to use these words as a prayer of thankfulness to God, asking him, day by day, to make them more and more real to you: 'How great is the love the Father has lavished on us, that we should be called children of God! And that is what we are!' (1 John 3.1).

Love that's for real

How do we know that love is for real? 'I love ice cream.' 'He loves the latest pop star, she the latest fashion.' 'They fell in and out of love in the blink of an eye.' Hasn't the word become misused to mean self-centred enjoyment, feeling good, emotionally excited – real, in so far as it goes, for a short time? But what about the love of a mother caring for her profoundly disabled child for decades on end? What about the person who risks his own life to save someone else's?

I knew John a little at university, as part of a large group of friends. He irritated me so much that I asked God to help me improve my attitude towards him! After university I moved to Surrey and we ended up in the same church where everyone assumed we were going out. I was having none of it. I wasn't nice to him, certainly didn't encourage a relationship. Then I fell ill, ended up back with my parents, unable to continue with my new life and career. John kept phoning and driving miles to visit, though I looked terrible and acted grumpy. Finally it dawned on me that this guy's love for me – unselfish, beyond price – didn't waver, even though he'd seen me at my worst. That's proved a solid foundation on which to build our future together! When the Bible says that God is love it means that reliable, lasting, unselfish, closely-involved-in-good-times-and-bad kind of love. In other words, real love. 'We know and rely on the love God has for us. God is love. Whoever lives in love lives in God, and God in him' (1 John 4.16).

John showed me the unselfish quality of his love by phoning and visiting while I was ill. Jesus shows me that his love is real in many ways but supremely in that he died for me. My parents are Christians. I'd known God, chatted away to him since early childhood, felt his love warming me sometimes. Aware he'd sent his Son Jesus to die on the cross for me, shortly before university I realized just how much that love cost him. When I heard someone speak about what he had suffered on the cross, Jesus' physical agonies seemed the most 'real' to me at first. Later that evening I understood that they formed perhaps the least of his sufferings. The shame of enduring his death agonies displayed on a very public gibbet, the pain of friends' desertion, even betrayal, and of unjust accusations coming from those claiming to worship his Father, the torture of feeling cut off from his amazingly close relationship with that Father as Jesus bore the consequences of all the evil in the world – all this was inflicted by the very people whom he'd left the splendours of heaven to help. Real love costs everything; real love lasts to death and beyond.

The letter to the Hebrews 12.2 says: 'Let us fix our eyes on Jesus, the author and perfecter of our faith, who for the joy set before him endured the cross, scorning its shame, and sat down at the right hand of the throne of God.' What was that joy, I wondered, which could carry the man who was God through such an experience? Not heaven, or he would never have come to earth in the first place. No, it was the joy of knowing that his enduring the cross would re-establish the relationship between God and human beings – with you and me. That's real love – and gives us, strange as it may seem, real hope.

Grace and kindness make me cry and I cried and cried that night. It had all seemed so cosy, my relationship with God.

I saw now that it was anything but. It hadn't come cheap and easy, not to him. I needed to take this relationship-beyond-price much more seriously. I responded to his total commitment to loving me much as I responded later to John's. I was sorry that I'd taken Jesus' love for granted, praying for things I wanted as though he were some genie bent on granting me not three but countless wishes. I needed to respond to his evident, overwhelming love with a committed love of my own – and not one where I called all the shots.

This wasn't when I found faith, or 'became a Christian'. It was one of the clear times when I grew up a bit – though even now I don't understand the half of what Jesus did on the cross, for me and for anyone who responds to his love.

Alex Mowbray has written a poem he's called 'Holy Hands', which sums up some of what I'm trying to say.

> Holy hands,
> hands with holes in,
> sinews stretched taut,
> wide,
> embracing the world he came to save,
> a world who loved then hated him –
> within one week the mood had changed
> reducing promised liberator to a powerless freak.
> We cannot measure yet
> all Christ accomplished on that cross
> but we can glimpse it,
> know the rest by faith.
> Through hands outstretched
> death has been nailed for good;
> by virtue of his sacrifice
> we are released;
> our spirits are set free
> inhabiting eternity.

Do read the account of Jesus' crucifixion for yourself in one of the four Gospels.

Spirited beginnings

I seem to be telling the story of how I found God to be real by going backwards in time . . .

Shortly before I'd understood how extraordinary was Jesus' love as shown on the cross, I'd arrived a day late on a weekend house party arranged for my church's youth group. Over lunch a friend asked if I'd come with her to an optional get-together about the Holy Spirit. I'd no idea what that meant but, having nothing else to do, said yes. Our curate and the guest speaker read and briefly explained some bits from the Bible about the Holy Spirit – the third person in the mysterious Trinity who makes up God. Might they pray for us to be filled with this Holy Spirit?

They made their way around the circle, quietly praying for those who wanted them to – but well before they reached me I found myself engulfed by overwhelming joy, like nothing I'd experienced before. It didn't leave me for months, despite the unremitting slog of A-level studies. Even school assemblies came alive as this Holy Spirit sprang out of every bit that was read from the Bible. Goodness, he'd been there, right from the beginning of the Old Testament! He 'was hovering over the waters' when the earth was still 'formless', 'empty' and 'dark' (Genesis 1.1–2). As with the proverbial elephant in the room, I'd never noticed him, let alone got to know him as a God-person, as I had with the Father and Jesus. But now this Holy Spirit was bringing the Bible and the other two persons of the Trinity even more alive to me. Jesus promised his disciples that the Holy Spirit 'will teach you all things and will remind you of everything I have said to you' (John 14.26).

Less than two years later I embarked on a degree in English literature and theology. I'm sure theology is taught better these days, but my course was deathly dull. The Holy Spirit brought the Bible alive: these lecturers could kill it! But they didn't kill it for me because I'd seen the reality of Jesus' love on the cross and experienced the joy and closeness of the Holy Spirit in my life. Not to mention lives of other Christians at the university who acted as though it were all true and found that it was. Were they or my lecturers more 'real'? No contest!

After he was raised from the dead, suddenly Jesus appeared among his disciples. They were cowering in a locked room, in fear for their own lives and in deep shock after the events of his trial and execution. Later, before he left this world, he told them something was going to change: 'You will receive power when the Holy Spirit comes on you; and you will be my witnesses in Jerusalem, and in all Judea and Samaria, and to the ends of the earth' (Acts 1.8). Their behaviour when he was with them for three years had hardly been promising; their state of mind after his death was even less so and now they weren't ever going to see Jesus again. Yet after the Holy Spirit 'came upon them', they changed utterly and preached the good news about Jesus to thousands of people out on the streets. Empowered, those men and women were now prepared to live to the full and even to die for him. You can find the story in Acts 2 onwards. Consider the implications if it is true that the Holy Spirit still loves to make himself, the Father and the Son real to us, teaching us more about them – changing and empowering us too.

Try it out!

Retired engineer Roger Madge became a Christian about half-way through his life. I didn't know him then but have seen his relationship with God grow deeper and stronger over the 20 or so years I have known him, so I asked him about it. This is what he said:

I guess you try it out, don't you? A bit like trying out a rickety-looking chair before trusting your weight to it. You might push on it in a few places, see if your hand goes through. If all's well you might balance one cheek on it while keeping most of your weight on your feet, then try wriggling about a bit. Eventually you commit to relaxing and letting the chair bear your weight properly.

Having a relationship with God means you end up changing your direction, your whole mindset. But with love or faith or anything like that it's the same, you test it out before pressing in further and further. Take praying. At first you feel really stupid, like you're talking to the wall – but if you don't start by doing that you'll never know whether or not there's a God who will hear you. So you try it out and sooner or later you experience something of God, or things happen as a result of your prayer. Some write them off as coincidence, but if you keep going and 'coincidences' keep happening, you begin to believe you're not just talking to a wall. Then you realize that to enter into any relationship with God it's the same as relating with another human being, you need two-way conversation. So you'd better start listening as well as talking.

When you first try that out you're likely to feel even more foolish – suppose you really are listening to a wall? But plenty of people have 'heard' God without having a relationship with him. If someone has even the beginnings of such a relationship, even if God still does appear like a wall at times, I can tell you from experience that he or she *will* 'hear' him. Not audibly – but there will be a distinct impression, a picture will form in your mind, or maybe a single word or phrase will emerge. And then you'll need to believe that its source isn't your imagination, nor the wall, but God. In other words, hearing him and having a two-way conversation is much easier than we think. He's ready to speak if we're ready to listen.

The next step involves taking action – doing what he says – because relationships that are all talk and no action don't go far. As we risk action we realize that we really can trust him.

Another thing – if we learn to listen to him before asking him for things, praying becomes much easier because we know what to ask for. Some people listen in quiet daily prayer, others while walking or engaged in everyday activities. But if we don't listen first, we might ask him for something which would be bad for us – or for someone else. Then, if in his mercy he doesn't give it to us, we might start doubting him.

I asked – having benefited from his prayers over the years – how all that affects the way Roger prays for people. He said:

I find it easier to pray for strangers, because then the things I know about someone don't get in the way of what God is saying. But, whether I've met someone previously or not, I try to listen to God, rather than to them or to my own opinions. Sometimes he tells me things about them, good or bad. My job isn't to direct people, nor to judge them in any way. My job is to encourage and build them up. So if I don't hear anything else specific from God I go ahead and bless them, because I know God wants to bless. I might pray that they will see the majesty of God and feel his love around them. I might pray that his light will shine wherever there is darkness for them and that he will give them his peace. Often then the person will say, 'There's something we need to deal with.' They've just experienced God's purity, majesty, grace, forgiveness and acceptance. Now that they realize who they are in God's eyes, how much they are loved and what their contribution is, their priorities shift. They understand what is important and what needs ditching – and take action. As Romans 2.4 says, God's grace (or kindness) leads us towards repentance. Repentance means turning around and going his way rather than our own, changing our direction, our whole mindset. It's not that the Lord says, 'Stop doing this and then you can get to know me and I'll help you.' Instead he says,

'Talk to me, listen to me, get to know me, let me fill you with my love and then you'll find yourself wanting to change.'

Worth testing out?

Getting to know him

We absorb so many things which are untrue or only partly true. Like those texts Victorians placed over beds saying, 'Thou God watchest me'. He's not prying, not some celestial surveillance camera, watching only for bad behaviour so he can punish us. He's more like a caring parent watching over little ones. He doesn't shield us from everything, but he does father us. As we come to know him better the relationship becomes more two-way and less restricted on our side to the 'I want' toddler stage.

Maureen Chapman – a former nurse-missionary, hotelier and shopkeeper – is now retired and living in the Brecon Beacons. She writes of a time when, under pressure, she came to know God better through the prompting of other people:

I first came to know God as a loving Father in 1969. I was returning home by sea on leave of absence after four years as a nurse-missionary in Nepal. I had thought I knew God, but my time in the Himalayas had shown me I did not, despite having been to Bible College and reading my Bible every day. Physically exhausted and emotionally worn out, I had stopped praying because God did not appear to answer my prayers.

My journey home by sea would take about three months, including a two-week stop in Durban. At the guesthouse there I checked my finances and realized I had barely enough money to pay my bill. No point telling God about it, I thought. The next evening I was invited to show slides of Nepal to the other guests, all Christian workers who were leaving the next day. I mentioned nothing of my needs, yet early the following morning a departing guest knocked on my bedroom door, pressed a large sum of money into my hand and said, 'God told me to give you this.' I was stunned – and cried.

I met other friendly companions, bought much-needed clothes and footwear, took two excursions into Zululand and was asked to speak at three more meetings. On the day my ship sailed, I found my guesthouse bill had been paid. A wonderful send-off included a huge bunch of roses. In my cabin I found a large envelope, sent by internal shipping post, containing many letters from the UK – organized by a stranger who was to become my husband. We have been married over 40 years now and still experience God's loving care.

St Paul prayed that the Christians in Ephesus, having been adopted into God's family, should come to know and be filled with 'all the fulness of God'. It's worth meditating on and even praying his words for yourself and any you know who feel, at the moment, isolated or unloved.

> In him and through faith in him we may approach God with freedom and confidence.
>
> I ask you, therefore, not to be discouraged because of my sufferings for you, which are your glory. For this reason I kneel before the Father, from whom his whole family in heaven and on earth derives its name. I pray that out of his glorious riches he may strengthen you with power through his Spirit in your inner being, so that Christ may dwell in your hearts through faith. And I pray that you, being rooted and established in love, may have power, together with all the saints, to grasp how wide and long and high and deep is the love of Christ, and to know this love that surpasses knowledge – that you may be filled to the measure of all the fulness of God.   (Ephesians 3.12–19)

Trust

Because of all the suffering in the world and the terrible things which happen, often I hear people saying that God can't be real. If he is real either he lacks the power to change those things or he doesn't care.

Terrible things do happen. Christians aren't exempt – and nor, of course, was Jesus. No other god claims to have come to this earth to experience and bear suffering on our behalf, as Jesus did. The Father and Holy Spirit also suffered in allowing him to do so.

Nevertheless, many of Jesus' early followers were killed because they followed him. It's still happening. More Christians were slaughtered because of their faith in the twentieth century than in the 19 preceding ones.

Innocent people of any faith or none are caught up in wars, earthquakes, tsunamis, road accidents, or die young of horrible diseases or starvation. Humans are directly to blame for some of these things – and for others indirectly, in that we could have prevented them. Consider – what if people didn't hate each other, drove more carefully, or if medicine, food and clean water were more available to the developing world? For example, the international community had the technology, if not the will, to put warning systems in place before the infamous Boxing Day tsunami in 2004.

People blame God for failing to prevent terrible things outside of our control – but I believe he does stop many disasters. A recent letter to the editor of our local community association magazine came from a former resident who wrote that she was walking on our common as a child when 'a doodle bug nearly killed us. I am alive today because God intervened and the doodle bug blew up above our heads with all the debris falling around us in a circle and my mother, sister, brother and myself completely unharmed in any way. As I remember it blew out all the windows in the village.' This is so similar to a story told me over a year before.

I met Hildegard Weinrich in a hotel in Jersey. No longer young or in good health, at mealtimes she kept the entire table in fits of laughter with her entertaining stories. Many of them involved her adventurous life serving God in Africa. Later I found out that she is someone who really does pray without ceasing – has done all her life – that she's a nun (minus the uniform!) and that she's still involved in helping people in need. She told a remarkable story of how God protected her life.

It was 1946, in Germany, the year after the war ended. The bombing had stopped, but there had been massive destruction. Even the buildings which appeared to be standing were often mere crumbling facades.

At 13 years old it was my habit to attend church early every morning before going to school. One day, as I walked towards the church, praying as usual (I'd talk freely to God about every-thing), suddenly a three-storey house collapsed, falling all around me. A mother with her baby screamed and ran ahead. I heard the tremendous noise of the building falling but was so deep in prayer that only on arriving at church did I think, 'I should have been killed!'

So, before going to school, I returned to where I had been standing and saw that, in the exact spot where I had stopped, a one-metre diameter circle was free from any rubble, debris and even dust.

I felt totally held and protected. I couldn't prove what had happened, and my mother didn't believe me – but I can tell you it's one small example among many which showed me that God is real and that he loves me!

Warn those who are lazy, comfort those who are frightened, take tender care of those who are weak, and be patient with everyone. See that no one pays back evil for evil, but always try to do good to each other and to everyone else. Always be joyful. Always keep on praying. No matter what happens, always be thankful, for this is God's will for you who belong to Christ Jesus . . . May the

God of peace himself make you entirely pure and devoted to God; and may your spirit and soul and body be kept strong and blameless until that day when our Lord Jesus Christ comes back again. God, who called you to become his child, will do all this for you, just as he promised.   (1 Thessalonians 5.14–24, TLB)

It's good to know that, if we are devoted to God with all our hearts, we belong to him and he will keep our spirits, souls and bodies strong and blameless until we meet Jesus face to face – even if we die first. Until then he is able to keep us alive and well enough to fulfil all the plans he has for us on this earth.

Religion or relationship?

'You Samaritans worship what you do not know; we worship what we do know, for salvation is from the Jews. Yet a time is coming and has now come when the true worshippers will worship the Father in spirit and truth . . . God is spirit, and his worshippers must worship in spirit and in truth.'

(John 4.22–24)

It's ironic when people come together, ostensibly to worship a God who is all about relationships, and then fall out with each other. By Jesus' time some of those who had been part of the original 12 Jewish tribes were worshipping in a different place and way from the rest. These 'Samaritans' and the other Jews wouldn't speak to each other. Each kept to their own geographical territory. But Jesus ignored such boundaries. He spoke to all.

Then there's the problem of religious traditions becoming more important than relationships. Jesus found certain hyper-religious Jews using an arcane point of religious law to wriggle out of giving financial support to their own elderly parents. He said:

'Thus you nullify the word of God for the sake of your tradition.
You hypocrites! Isaiah was right when he prophesied about you:
"These people honour me with their lips, but their hearts are
far from me. They worship me in vain; their teachings are but
rules taught by men."'   (Matthew 15.6–9)

Some churches today can be cold, unloving and full of factions – terrible adverts for Christianity. There, you'd never guess
our faith's founder said: 'A new command I give you: Love one
another. As I have loved you, so you must love one another.
By this all men will know that you are my disciples' (John
13.34–35).

Clearly Jesus didn't want us to live out our faith solely in
relation to himself, the Father and the Holy Spirit, but to be in
a loving relationship with one another too. I think worship is
a bit like sex in that when people come together to express their
love in an intimate way it can be sublime. Gone wrong, as
in rape or child abuse, it's horrific. We become like a horrific
stench to God if we go through the motions of worshipping
him together while failing to love, respect and honour him or
one another. Worship isn't only about singing and praying on
Sundays, it's about how we live the rest of our lives. The word
means 'giving worth to' – and if we hold God in high regard
we'll do as he says.

No church is perfect, nor totally corrupt, so I hesitated
to tell the following story in which my own church appears
in a good light (believe me, it's not perfect!). Another church
appears in a less good light, although many within it serve
God faithfully and love others well. Given those riders, here
are the experiences of one young man who came to know God
and then discovered the extraordinary joy of church life and
relationships. They illustrate that, despite all the difficulties of
relating within groups, despite our individualistic society, God
is certainly alive, well – and very real – within churches.

When Heiner Georgi hit our church as a gap-year 'Time for God' volunteer we'd never seen anything quite like him! He arrived, aged 18, from what had been Communist East Germany. Within days he seemed to be known and loved by all 300 of us, so enthusiastic, outgoing, encouraging and full of energy was he, helping with church activities from youth work to humping tables around. Yet until I interviewed him for this book I'd not appreciated that he'd never felt part of a church in this way before.

Born a year and a half after the Berlin Wall came down, Heiner declared, aged three, that he wanted to be a Lutheran pastor, as had generations of his mother's family. At ten he chose ongoing education appropriate to this aim. The Communists had prevented his mother from doing likewise because she refused to join the Party, so she had trained as a physiotherapist and worked in the town's wonderful Lutheran Foundation for disabled children where her own father was Pastor.

Heiner's mother had prayed for him every day since his conception and his grandfather taught him many things about the faith. Heiner felt at home in the Foundation's chapel and is grateful for his Lutheran upbringing but found church services in the town boring and unfriendly. His schoolfriend Johannes's family had moved from a very different kind of church in Saxony and their lively relationship with Jesus attracted Heiner. But that family could find no church within miles of their new home where people expressed their love of Jesus together every day of the week, and were 'led by the Holy Spirit' rather than by tradition.

Heiner would read his Bible and talk with Johannes's mother every day before school. 'Have you given your life to the Lord, Heiner?' she asked him one day. Luther didn't mention anything like that, so Heiner found a prayer – on the Internet! 'Lord,

I know that I'm a sinner and that you died on the cross for me. I want to live for you now, to give everything to you.' He believed – but still didn't *feel* that his relationship with Jesus had come alive.

Knowing Heiner needed something more than he could find from the local Lutherans, Johannes's mother told him about a large church in Karlsruhe, 350 miles away, which broadcast its services on TV at 8 o'clock every Saturday morning. At 15, Heiner lapped these up and, later, many others via the Internet. Eventually he managed to visit the Karlsruhe church three times. People there worshipped Jesus with great joy and freedom, the way he'd done in front of the computer screen – but this was far better. Then the senior pastor, who knew not even his name, told Heiner, 'The Holy Spirit is saying you are called to ministry.'

From that point on, Heiner felt he was in a real conversation with God whenever he prayed or read the Bible at home. He worshipped sometimes with Johannes's family and, as he was 17 by then, started asking God about what he should do after school. To cut a very long story short, he applied to do a gap year with 'Time for God' in England and ended up in our church. Despite his extremely limited church experience and the language and cultural differences, he took to it like the proverbial duck to water. 'I love it because not only are there lively services and good teaching but people are friendly and hospitable, unlike in churches at home. I see the Holy Spirit working and I'm learning such a lot.' Heiner knows that God wants him to take all of the life and love he is experiencing back to his area of Germany, and so our church is sponsoring him to stay on for a while to study towards gaining theological qualifications for ministry.

It's good to pray for churches, that God's vibrant life and big-hearted love will flourish within congregations, spilling out into the communities around. Lord, help each one of us to worship in spirit and in truth and to grow in our love of one another and of you.

Belonging, loved

We're looking at relationships, with God and with people, in this section. Ever noticed that some individuals back off, taking offence or misunderstanding easily, however friendly and welcoming people are towards them? Perhaps they were so hurt as children that they've been carrying around a huge load of rejection ever since. Prickly people end up lonely. Present-day misunderstandings and perceived offences only make them wear defensive armour which weighs them down even more.

People are fallible – whether we mean to or not, we do let each other down, which means that none of us has escaped hurt in life. If someone triggers a hurtful memory, even if it remains within my subconscious, I know I can react out of all proportion. Unless we take steps to stop our hurt colouring everything, at every recurrence life appears a shade or two darker. When a sense of rejection gains the upper hand, we cease to love ourselves – and so it becomes impossible to love anyone else. Yet Jesus said there are only two things in life which we need to do: 'Love the Lord your God with all your heart and with all your soul and with all your mind and with all your strength', and 'Love your neighbour as yourself' (Mark 12.30–31).

Perhaps we need first of all to know that God loves us, whoever we are, whatever we do – and to receive that love from him as a gift. He's the only one who has known me from before I was born, right through my life to date, and who will still be with me until and beyond death. I don't deserve his love, I don't know why he loves me, but I do know that he does. His Son Jesus proved it when he died for me – and for you.

If God sees me as loveable it's surely ungracious to tell him, 'No I'm not – you're a liar!' Likewise, if he sees you as loveable, it's ungracious of me not to love you too. If we let God's love provide a secure bedrock for all our other relationships, we can remember that God loves and accepts us when we're let down and rejected by people. We can let go of the pain before it damages us – colours our vision dark, adds to our load, our prickliness, misery . . . whatever. I love these words from God written down by an ancient Hebrew prophet: 'Can a mother forget the baby at her breast and have no compassion on the child she has borne? Though she may forget, I will not forget you! See, I have engraved you on the palms of my hands' (Isaiah 49.15–16).

A little later the song-writer king, David, recorded a kind of conversation between his soul and God:

> My heart says of you, 'Seek his face!' Your face, LORD, I will seek. Do not hide your face from me, do not turn your servant away in anger; you have been my helper. Do not reject me or forsake me, O God my Saviour. Though my father and mother forsake me, the LORD will receive me.
>
> (Part of Psalm 27 – it's worth reading the rest to see how David's relationship with the Lord worked.)

Teenager Jack Lu told me about a time when he felt rejected and lost his way a bit. He was in 'The Tribe', a church group intended for 11–13s, as was correct for his actual age. But all his friends had gone up to the 14–18s (known as The Group). Jack felt left out. He became increasingly critical and miserable, avoiding most church activities until, one day, a visitor to the church handed him one piece of a jigsaw puzzle. She didn't know him or his problems but told him, 'I believe God wants you to know that you're part of the picture.' That same day Jack heard that another person, younger than himself, was being allowed to move up to The Group. Should he feel jealous and miserable about that, or accept the encouragement that God understood him and wanted him as part of the picture? He chose the latter and asked God's forgiveness for his own negative and critical attitudes. Later that day he received the news that he'd also been invited to join The Group.

Less than a year on, Jack told me:

> I've come to understand that I am a pretty selfish person. Most of the time I pray only when I need or want something for myself. I've had to learn that's a very one-sided relationship! Yet wherever I go, I know I'll never be appreciated like God appreciates me. Even when people used to appreciate me I'd find it hard to appreciate myself. But God knows and understands me like no other. You know in the story of Jesus' trial and crucifixion, when they spat at him and he forgave them? Jesus said, 'They don't understand what they are doing.' Well, reading about that I felt the love Jesus had for them – for us! And now I look at all the people around me and think how much God appreciates them and understands what each of them is going through. I try to do the same now – to show compassion and not judge others. I like to people-watch, trying to understand people like Jesus did – and does. I would love to be more like him all the time.

Jesus was despised and rejected – without reacting badly, still loving, still forgiving. He bore all that rejection and pain so that we don't have to – and so that we can relate well to him and to each other.

A real family

I find my sense of observation sharper when I'm away from familiar things, which may be why it struck me how God is for real in others particularly while I was in Ghana, West Africa.

As a timid young Surrey housewife I spent three weeks there, researching my first book.

Beforehand I'd felt completely out of my depth at the very thought of visiting somewhere quite 'off my map'. I'd need to question and understand people of a completely different culture and language group. Before leaving, I was briefed on what not to do. For example, 'Don't pass food with your left hand – that's reserved for wiping your bottom. Don't cross your legs – and in particular, don't point your toes at anyone, it's seen as the height of rudeness.'

I was writing about a church, founded by a man from the UK, which was now entirely African. Early on, I attended its huge outdoor Easter conference in the capital, Accra. Loudspeakers in different areas relayed the proceedings in different West African languages, while I was assigned personal translators. I knew very few of the songs but found it surprisingly easy to worship God, along with everyone around me: I could see the love of God in their faces.

I couldn't make out where the congregation ended, so far did it stretch on three sides of a huge square space. In its centre, lines of women danced with African grace, twirling white handkerchiefs in honour of their Lord and sometimes 'sweeping' the ground before him with colourful cloths, as they would to honour an earthly chief. On the final day, my translator prevailed upon me to join the dance line. Afterwards I watched a video of conference highlights and – oh no, the camera zoomed in on my ungainly hops and then on the women behind, who abandoned their graceful movements to imitate me! Oh the embarrassment – and, later, the laughter!

That kind of imitation is not what it's all about. Happily, to this day, that Ghanaian church has kept its own culture while maintaining the absolute truth of its relationship with Jesus. No counterfeits or pale imitations here – only African life and vigour! Later I spent several hours interviewing five people who had been with this church since its struggling beginnings. They had few material possessions – and Ghana had experienced near-famine not so many years previously. Yet they radiated, to a degree I've seen rarely before or since, such peace, love, joy, confidence in the Lord, together with practical concern for others.

By the end, our conversation morphed seamlessly into prayer and I was in tears. Why had I been so worried? God was here, overflowing these people – the same God whom I know, the same values, the same love – only more so. We really were part of the same family – the resemblances obvious despite differences in skin colour, wealth, education, history, culture and language. None of those things mattered – knowing God did.

Before he was crucified, Jesus prayed, first for the close friends he was leaving and then, in the passage below, for all who love and follow him – including us.

> 'My prayer is not for them alone. I pray also for those who will believe in me through their message, that all of them may be one, Father, just as you are in me and I am in you. May they also be in us so that the world may believe that you have sent me. I have given them the glory that you gave me, that they may be one as we are one: I in them and you in me. May they be brought to complete unity to let the world know that you sent me and have loved them even as you have loved me.'

(John 17.20–23)

Some would say that Jesus' prayer has not been answered, citing the disgraceful splits and even violence between different Christian factions, throughout history. Yet many have worked together and been 'one in spirit', recognizing and loving Jesus in one another, as happened between me and those Africans. Being good news – living in peace, love and co-operation – doesn't make headlines or history books. But it is real. In

England, the denominational divides which kept different 'flavours' of Christian apart a generation or two ago simply don't any more – and most are happy with any church where people love and serve the Lord.

I've known Elizabeth Hudson for about 15 years, during which she's worked tirelessly alongside members of several churches in our village and area. She writes:

Over the years, I have seen God at work in many different people, from a wide variety of backgrounds and denominations. Rich diversity reflects something of the many facets of God, who never confines himself to one type of church! As with any family, there are differences, but more unites us as Christians than divides us, for our common strong bond is that God loves us all.

As daughter of a Congregational minister I was given a good knowledge of Bible stories, of God and of his Son, Jesus. Later, as mother of two young children, I found myself living briefly in The Hague, Holland, and became involved in both the Anglican and Roman Catholic communities (the only two English-speaking churches there). Through those Christians I understood that God was for real. They introduced me to the third member of the Trinity – the Holy Spirit. My two-dimensional notion of God and Jesus from those early Bible-story days took on that vital third dimension as the three persons of the Trinity seemed to jump out of the pages of the Bible, coming alive for me.

Returning to Cheshire, my faith continued to grow with good teaching in a Methodist church until, after another house move, I found my present spiritual home in a Baptist one. Here I'm committed to working with the different churches in our local community. We see ourselves as a Christian family who come together regularly to pray and to worship, as well as to plan and prepare practical contributions to village life, such as innovative youth provision, in this age of local authority cutbacks. The churches, working with our local traders, also facilitate and organize the late-night Christmas opening of shops early in December – an important date in our village's calendar. The whole community – young and old, churchgoers or not – loves to join together in a celebration renowned for the warmest of atmospheres, whatever the weather.

A visit to Khartoum in 2000 confirmed to me how God is interested in people, not labels. Those Sudanese Christians, with no denominational tag attached, met and worshipped under huge difficulties in an Arab Muslim state. Displaced from the south by civil war, they lived in shanty towns on the edge of Khartoum. They had so little, yet gave all of it to us – their great joy and love, the only three plastic chairs available for the service and afterwards a bottle of Coke to refresh us as they made music and danced for us. God was very real to them. I found it a humbling experience.

If you've only come across one 'flavour' of Christian, try to talk and maybe to worship with others. Find out about how churches are working together in your area and get involved. God loves all the branches of his family, but you might fit with one better than another, so try out different churches until you find one which fits with you. Maybe you have a part to play in fulfilling Jesus' amazing prayer for all his followers, in your local area.

Worship

Our adolescent son couldn't understand why God wanted people to praise and worship him all the time. Wasn't that big-headed, a bit of an ego-trip?

Good question. I don't believe God needs our worship. He is perfect, complete – totally secure within himself. But I do believe that worshipping God changes us and helps to develop our relationship with him.

It has parallels with human marriage, which wouldn't be much if the partners didn't ever express their love for one another, in word and deed. Worship is our love-language to God. That's if we worship him in spirit and in truth. As we've seen with Heiner's story, far more than singing and praying together on Sundays, true worship involves our hearts and souls, our lives and behaviour all week. It means putting God first – literally, giving him 'worth'.

The 'basic ingredients' of a relationship with God or with another human being are similar to the ones I've used for the headings of this book: beginnings, helping one another, communication, changing in the light of that relationship, surviving times when we question or doubt one another, and 'outworking' – letting all that's good in our relationship benefit others too. Worship is different. When one person starts worshipping another, normally it spells t-r-o-u-b-l-e. No one is perfect. Human beings will let their worshippers down. Or the worshipper becomes obsessional about the person – a footballer or rock star perhaps. 'Get a life!' we say, 'Don't live it through someone else!'

But if we give God worth and live our lives through him, then we will be able to extend his love to others.

I asked my friend, retired medical data manager Ann Stringer, what difference worshipping God had made to her relationship with him.

I have been actively involved in various churches throughout my life, although sometimes I missed services as I was helping with their children's work. Later I enjoyed singing in a church choir – but by then my youngest child was the only teenager at that church so we decided to try elsewhere. It so happened that the building of the church we tried was being refurbished, so they were meeting temporarily in our village's primary school hall.

From the start the worship there hit me, transforming my relationship with God. He felt close there, as though part of me, instead of some mystical being up in the sky. The worship was personal and accessible – partly because the children's paintings on the walls placed us in the midst of an everyday community. It made me think about how I had been worshipping God. Did I really believe in him or was I just hedging my bets, going to church out of habit and saying words I'd learnt by rote? I changed. Now I could worship God anywhere, any time. So, for example, I will sit on a bench when I walk my dogs to pray and worship God, something I would never have done before. Worshipping him feels such a natural response – both with other people and on my own.

Two years later we all went away for a church weekend together. As we worshipped, singing 'I surrender' to God, again something hit me. I had to sit down very suddenly in case I fell. I could no longer keep any part of my life back from God, so I said, 'I'm yours, all of me, whatever it takes, whatever you require.' He's the Lord, he's the boss – and that's fine because he loves me, loves all of us.

Whether it's in song with others or in quiet reflection alone, I need to express my awe and love and worship. I'd never have got through the last six years which have brought all kinds of family problems – including the death of my husband and my own breast cancer – without worshipping. It does something deep inside me, encouraging me to get to know this amazing God better and acting like a healing balm.

I'm sure Ann is right. Worship changes your perspective, helps you see who's in charge and how amazing he is. Recently we visited Knockan Crag in the bleak and spectacular northern Highlands of Scotland. There geologists first realized that young rocks could appear below older ones – from that discovery the theory of plate tectonics would develop. An interpretative trail at Knockan includes a great man-made globe of layered rock.

At the bottom corner of my photo of that globe is the lonely road with a few parked cars, far below. In that empty, majestic landscape, so absurdly tiny did those cars appear that I thought of the God's-eye view expressed in Isaiah 40.22–23: 'He sits enthroned above the circle of the earth, and its people are like grasshoppers. He stretches out the heavens like a canopy, and spreads them out like a tent to live in. He brings princes to naught and reduces the rulers of this world to nothing.' He's 'out of this world' – and yet he's with us!

I also thought of Brian Cox, the professor whose inspiring documentaries about the formation and workings of the universe are so full of awe, wonder and beauty. He's an atheist and presumably pours all that awe into practising and communicating science. That's great, as far as it goes – though science can't be the answer to everything and has had bad consequences for the world as well as good.

By contrast I find myself thinking, 'Wow, even though my brain can't understand the millionth of it, I know the all-powerful God who made all that – and he loves me!' I believe, like Ann, that worshipping God is a natural part of the way we're meant to function – it's what to do with the awe and wonder we all feel – and it's transforming. If such an amazing God is at the centre of our lives (and true worship implies that), then everything else – all our fears and worries, all the things that are wrong within and outside of us, together with our material wealth or lack of it – fall into perspective.

Talking of a change of perspective, you might like to reflect on these words from Psalm 73, written by a man fretting about baddies getting away with murder. Worship changes his way of thinking as he sees things from a God's-eye view.

> When I tried to understand all this, it was oppressive to me till I entered the sanctuary of God . . . When my heart was grieved and my spirit embittered, I was senseless and ignorant; I was

a brute beast before you. Yet I am always with you; you hold me by my right hand. You guide me with your counsel, and afterwards you will take me into glory. Whom have I in heaven but you? And earth has nothing I desire besides you. My flesh and my heart may fail, but God is the strength of my heart and my portion for ever. Those who are far from you will perish; you destroy all who are unfaithful to you. But as for me, it is good to be near God. I have made the Sovereign LORD my refuge; I will tell of all your deeds.   (Psalm 73.16–17, 21–28)

Help

When young Australian Aborigines go 'walkabout' for several weeks or months, the idea behind their wandering is that, away from the security of home, they learn to trust the land to sustain and protect them. Happily most of us don't need to desert our families to try out our trust in God and find out whether or not he is real.

Help me!

Anne Rasmussen writes of a time when God intervened suddenly to help her:

> I had not been feeling well for some months but, with a baby to care for, I didn't take too much notice of myself. Then, one night, I awoke with violent stomach pains, was rushed into hospital and found to have an ovarian cyst and stomach infection. Following surgery, I made no progress towards recovery and for a week became so ill with continuing nausea that I could neither eat nor drink. As I became weaker I wondered if I would die.
>
> The decision was made to pump out my stomach, but in my weakened state I could not swallow the plastic tubes. An intimidating doctor and ward sister implied that I was being awkward. When they walked off, saying they would return shortly for another attempt, I reached my low point and called out in despair to God. I think I cried simply, 'Help me!'
>
> Words from the Bible sprang vividly into my mind. They were from Isaiah 43.1 (RSV):

Fear not, for I have redeemed you;
I have called you by name, you are mine.
When you pass through the waters I will be with you;
And through the rivers, they shall not overwhelm you.

It was as if God was in that hospital ward speaking directly to me, telling me not to be afraid – all would be well, and I would get better. To my amazement, at once I felt a little stronger and knew that this was a turning point in my illness – so, when another doctor arrived to perform the dreaded intervention, I had the courage to say firmly, 'I don't need it as I am feeling better.'

I didn't tell him what had happened to me. Perhaps I should have done. But that doctor agreed to delay any further intervention until the following day, by which time I didn't need it. I'd begun to drink, and then to eat small amounts. When I'd called out to God in my desperately weakened state, he had reached out and healed me, of that I was convinced. I recovered rapidly and a few days later was discharged from hospital. It happened many years ago, but I still remember that time when God spoke so vividly to me when I called out to him in my need.

You can call that a coincidence. You can call it psychological – if Anne's fears were calmed by those words from the Bible, maybe her stomach calmed down. Or maybe that was the mechanism God used. After all, why did those particular words come to her so suddenly? If it had been some random thought, why would she feel calm and know that God was speaking to her, assuring her that all would be well?

How did God heal her? I don't know. Anne doesn't know. But she does know that he spoke to her, comforted and reassured her when she felt all alone in a frightening situation – and that in a remarkably short time she was well again. Not the biggest miracle in the world, but a miracle nonetheless – a sign of God's love that has encouraged Anne subsequently, as she's faced other difficult situations.

The words from the prophet Isaiah, through which God spoke to Anne, first applied to the people of ancient Israel. If God could rescue, sustain and heal a whole nation through all kinds of difficulties and hurts, he can do the same for us now. We may have to pass through some rough waters but he will be right there with us. Even if he does not intervene directly, he will strengthen us and not let us be overwhelmed.

If God would send his angels

When I asked an assortment of Christians how they knew God was for real, quite a few came up with angel stories. The word 'angel' means 'messenger', and a number appear in the Bible – often looking like ordinary people rather than awesome beings from the sky. These words from the Bible explain a little more:

> He will command his angels concerning you to guard you in all your ways. (Psalm 91.11)

> Are not all angels ministering spirits sent to serve those who will inherit salvation? (Hebrews 1.14)

> Do not forget to entertain strangers, for by so doing some people have entertained angels without knowing it. (Hebrews 13.2)

I've chosen three true stories. They prove nothing – the 'angels' could be particularly shy but helpful human beings. But they do indicate that God sometimes sends special messengers in answer to our prayers – signs that he really does care about us.

Rosie Berry from Hertfordshire wrote:

> I shall never forget the sickening feeling that cold wet November day when all the electrics cut out on my old Allegro

just as it reached a roundabout. Streams of traffic passed sneeringly. With my young daughter in the car I needed help fast and turned to my favourite quick prayer: 'Oh Lord, help!'

Through the battering rain I noticed that we were being overtaken by a cheerful yellow BT van. To my surprise it pulled up on the pavement ahead. A man came towards me; he had an authority about his manner. Together we pushed the car into a convenient lay-by.

Then he asked me, 'What about your daughter?'

I realized we were only a few steps from a Christian bookshop whose manager was a friend of mine. She agreed to look after Helena there until I could collect her.

Returning to my sad vehicle, I found the BT man offering me a phone card – he seemed to be a mind-reader. I turned to thank him, but he had vanished, so I thanked God for his intervention instead, for I was sure it had been divinely inspired. I can't pass that roundabout now without smiling at the answer to my urgent prayer.

Ken Bryan from Birmingham also wrote about an 'everyday' angel:

The day was bleak and colourless but my wife said, 'We must go to Sainsbury's or else we shall starve.'

I groaned.

Arriving at the supermarket, we each collected a trolley and took the travelator to the upper sales floor. Pat, my wife, was behind me with her trolley when I heard her cry out. Apparently she had grabbed at the handrail and missed. She fell backwards. Because of a previous injury, this could have been very serious. I heard a voice say, 'Don't worry. I've got you and I won't let you go.' I looked and saw Pat being supported by a big man with black skin. We arrived at the top and the man asked Pat if she was all right. She said that she was and the man went into the store.

We followed, but he was nowhere to be seen. Although we looked all around, to thank him properly, we couldn't find him again. Was he an angel? I think so. God is good and he is always there for us.

Teacher Roma Bell wrote:

A few years ago I was on a skiing holiday with a group of about 60 Christians. Jim, one of the group, didn't appear for dinner. When there was still no word from him by the evening meeting we were all concerned and prayed for his safety. About the time the meeting finished he rejoined us and told the following story. Jim had decided to walk rather than ski in the mountains that day, taking the opportunity of fine weather to enjoy the spectacular scenery. He had with him his day-rucksack, a packed lunch and a piste map, and wore a ski jacket, sturdy shoes, gloves, hat and sunglasses.

He enjoyed exploring the paths and seeing the mountain from a different perspective but, after lunch, the clear blue sky turned grey and it started snowing. The wind whipped up and blew the snow, changing the landscape and making it increasingly difficult for him to see the path. As visibility reached white-out conditions, Jim's anxiety increased. He had lost his way. To stray in that terrain could be fatal – and soon darkness began to fall.

Jim could not hear a sound. He stopped, prayed and thought about what he should do. Going on was madness, so he started to dig a hole in which to take shelter until morning. No food left, no extra clothes – would he survive the night on the mountain?

As he was digging, something attracted his attention. Stopping and peering through the darkness Jim realized that a man was waving at him – the first human he had seen for hours. Jim shouted but no sound came back. Instead the man waved again and then beckoned. Jim moved towards him but the man didn't stop to wait for him, he carried on walking – fast if Jim hurried, slower when Jim slowed down. He seemed skilful at picking out a safe path. They carried on down the mountainside like this for some time before Jim noticed that his guide had left no footprints in the freshly fallen snow. Looking back, Jim could see but one set – his own.

Eventually Jim reached a minor road and a clear way forward. As soon as his feet touched the road his guide disappeared. Soon Jim came to a small house where lights were on. He rushed to knock at the door and was welcomed inside. His hosts phoned our chalet to say he was safe and then kindly drove him over to us. Jim walked in just as the meeting was finishing and when he told us his story you could have heard a pin drop.

This poor man called, and the LORD heard him; he saved him out of all his troubles. The angel of the LORD encamps around those who fear him, and he delivers them. Taste and see that the LORD is good; blessed is the man who takes refuge in him.

(Psalm 34.6–8)

People don't have to be in deep trouble, or meet an angel to 'taste and see that the LORD is good'. But I think those who told the 'ordinary angel' stories above would urge anyone to do just that.

Be still and know

God is our refuge and strength, an ever-present help in trouble. Therefore we will not fear, though the earth give way and the mountains fall into the heart of the sea, though its waters roar and foam and the mountains quake with their surging . . . Be still, and know that I am God.   (Psalm 46.1–3, 10)

Joan Mason-Martin is a retired teacher from Torquay who loves writing poetry. In the time I've known her, old age has made Joan increasingly frail but, although she lives alone, little appears to daunt her. I wondered why and asked her to write about how she experiences reality within her relationship with God.

I haven't seen a blinding light or heard a clear voice. I can sense God speaking to me, though – with comforting, loving words. 'I have called you by name, you are mine.' 'I am with you always.'

Though I didn't perhaps realize it at the time, he sustained me during my mother's last illness. I've prayed too when worried about my own health or a journey taken alone. He hasn't healed me completely or made the journey free from problems but it could have been much worse. Somehow there will always be a kind helper. For example, I was told Battle was an unmanned station and wondered anxiously how I was going to carry my case up and over its bridge to the exit. As I stood there, a young schoolgirl offered to carry it. I tried to phone for a taxi – then one appeared.

I feel close to God in nature. When I see a wonderful view of sea and sky, glowing flowers, brilliant butterflies, the variety of colours and shapes in leaves, then tears of joy and wonder rise up in me.

I know he's always there. I can always talk to him, ask for forgiveness and strength, and I can, with confidence, place others in his care.

Joan's quiet trust in God is rooted in decades of experience – that he knows and loves her, will help her, and is there, all of the time. It's not only amid desperate, dramatic situations that God helps us, but in quiet 'ordinary' ways. Only by stopping and being still a moment will we 'know' that he is God. Realizing that we have a relationship with the one who made those leaves and butterflies lifts our hearts, giving us confidence as well as joy. Especially when he then whispers something like, 'I am with you always, to the very end of the age' (Matthew 28.20).

The kindness of strangers can depend on location. Among the hurrying crowds of central London you might expect it to be less forthcoming than, say, in a rural Sussex station like Battle. Yet an elderly friend of my mother's, needing a London clinic's treatment for her debilitating condition, found a stranger stopped to help whenever she needed an arm to assist her up a long flight of steps out of the nearest Underground. 'Each time at the bottom of the steps I stood still and prayed,' she said. 'I was totally helpless, yet, without fail, within a moment or two, help appeared.'

They say that a problem shared is a problem halved. Within any relationship of love and trust, it helps so much to be able to talk. We can tell God our worries, confess our shortcomings and weaknesses and ask for his strength, his aid. We don't have to, of course. We can hit the panic button, run around like headless chickens or assert our independence and try to sort everything out by ourselves. But I find things much easier when I remember to be still for a moment, consider that God is a lot better at this sort of thing than I am, and ask for his help.

It's less likely that he'll work a big miracle than that we'll find that, once calmer, we see what to do. God may point us in the direction of someone who could help, or simply lend us the strength to endure. Whatever happens, God and not our own problems or frailties have become our centre of gravity, our still centre. We're anything but alone – and that makes all the difference.

Knowing the sense of hearing is one of the last things to go, I read Psalm 46 at the hospital bedside of someone we loved who was unconscious and, we were told, unlikely to recover. Her favourite psalm, it had comforted her when her own mother was dying. Amazingly, as I write, she is fully conscious and increasingly mobile. Though she can remember nothing of the time she was so seriously ill, apart from 'horrid dreams', I'm glad I read the psalm. If nothing else, it helped me. And, despite my being interrupted several times as doctors and nurses came to do what they could for her, it helped us feel the presence of God in that busy clinical assessment unit.

Trusting in God when you're in a tight spot may not feel very safe, especially at first. But then neither did taking my feet off the bottom of the swimming pool and trusting that the water would support me during childhood swimming lessons. Today I know that if I lay my head back onto the water, relax and let my legs drift upwards, unlikely as it seems, I'll soon be floating on my back. Although I'm a worrier and do still spin into panic mode, at least I've plenty of experience of times when God, like the water, has supported me, never letting me down. What about you? Can you take your feet off the bottom and begin to trust him, even if you never have done so before? You'll find 'swimming' with him is great, once you get the hang of it!

To blame or a help?

Retired teacher Robert Stephen grew up in a fishing village on the east coast of northern Scotland where many were devout Christians. He writes:

I attended church and Sunday school every week but saw God as a distant, judgemental being who 'kept an eye on me' in a way which seemed more frightening than reassuring. The village's many denominations didn't seem to get on well with each other – I didn't like that, either.

When I was 12 my father died of cancer. It had been a long, painful process following four years of poor health. No chemo in those days, only morphine from the village doctor, sometimes daily – it all happened under my nose in our small house.

So, what about God? He'd become unfair and unjust in my opinion – if he was there at all. I had friends whose still-alive dads drank and sometimes beat them; they never went to church. My God-fearing, good parents deserved better.

My mother received just ten shillings child allowance per week to support her two sons. But, being a woman of great resolve, she began her own business in the village and did her utmost to give us a good start in life. She retained her commitment to God and church through everything that happened, seeing to it that I continued with church and encouraging me to be a good example to my younger brother. All the time, though, I harboured simmering anger and anxiety towards God. Confused, I wondered – did he even exist?

Meanwhile, my father's cousin – we knew him as 'Uncle Tom' – had a splendid new boat built. Following the tradition of many Christian seamen locally, he named it from Scripture – *Quiet Waters*, from Psalm 23. Tom's son, brother and brother's son Robert were among the crew. When I was nearly 15, and Robert about two years older, Robert asked for the hymn 'Jesus, Saviour, pilot me' to be sung the evening they set sail. The fleet was caught in a storm on that trip and *Quiet Waters* never returned. Not one body was found, only driftwood. What a huge loss to our community – and to my family especially! I became even more angry with God.

So you might wonder why, at 17 years, I accepted Jesus Christ as my Saviour. During my angry years a number of things had impressed me greatly. I came to understand the value of many of Jesus' teachings. The accuracy of Old Testament prophecies about him amazed me, as did the way Christianity first spread through a few ordinary men. The tenacity of my mother's faith in the face of severe adversity, along with the many Christians in the village who showed us great kindness also impressed me. One day our elderly minister challenged me about faith and belief. When I walked away he was in tears. Why should the old geezer care about me?

Finally, I heard a sermon on 'Emotion, Intellect and Will'. The preacher stressed that people shouldn't become Christians through having warm fuzzy feelings about a God who could do them lots of good. That was certainly not my problem. 'Intellect' – OK, I reckoned I'd a good understanding and gave Christianity high marks out of ten. 'Will' – that meant confronting my hostility towards God over the death of my father. The preacher highlighted the injustice suffered by Jesus on the cross, where he was punished for people's sins, including mine. This left me with such an inner turmoil that I prayed for forgiveness. I found it hard, back then, to understand how the anger left me – I know now that it was the power of God's Holy Spirit. I was sure, aged 17, that I felt utterly different – and committed myself to following Jesus some weeks later. This I have gone on doing, with many failures when I haven't followed too closely. The intellectual bit is still OK for me, but grasping the extent and depths of God's love emotionally is a lifetime's journey.

The LORD is my shepherd, I shall not be in want. He makes me lie down in green pastures, he leads me beside quiet waters, he restores my soul. He guides me in paths of righteousness for his name's sake. Even though I walk through the valley of the shadow of death, I will fear no evil, for you are with me; your rod and your staff, they comfort me. You prepare a table before me in the presence of my enemies. You anoint my head with oil; my cup overflows. Surely goodness and love will follow me all the days of my life, and I will dwell in the house of the LORD for ever.   (Psalm 23)

Many people know and love that passage from the Bible about how God looks after his people as a good shepherd cares for his sheep. David, who wrote it, knew the realities of looking after silly sheep in a semi-desert – a rocky and tumultuous area. Quiet waters – any waters – weren't easy to find, nor was green grass, for most of the year. Sheep became entangled in thorns or fell down cliffs. Wolves and lions had to be fought off. Bandits lurking in shadowy valleys were partial to roast lamb and warlike tribes abounded. Life was cheap, stability rare.

There's little time for soul-restoring when survival is at stake – and yet David experienced God's goodness and help then and there. God doesn't make unrealistic promises that we'll stay by 'quiet waters' all the time. But he does restore our souls and spirits, even through life's storms or its dry and dangerous places. Enemies, evil, darkness, death and fear all make their appearance within this short psalm. But God being there with us makes all the difference. If we've learnt to trust him and know that he loves us, we're more likely to let him help us. Conversely, when something terrible happens, people who aren't sure whether he exists will often blame God – and it's hard to receive help from someone we hold to blame.

One Sunday, our church worshipped through a song which asks Jesus to be the centre of our lives and the wind which fills our sails. Along with the words, someone had projected a picture of a windmill. But its sails were mere wooden frameworks – even the strongest wind wouldn't have sent them spinning. In order to grind good flour, the miller would have had to rig something (like canvas) over them to catch the wind. I found myself praying this:

Lord, I can see you doing your bit – your powerful wind blows and is well able to magnify any good I do, so long as I rig and trim my 'sails' to catch the wind of your Holy Spirit. Help me to do that instead of fighting against you or blaming you for everything that goes wrong. Only then can you guide, comfort, restore and feed and help me do good. Only then can I prove how very real you are!

When troubles come 'in battalions'

Martin Kruger, retired but active in a Surrey church, writes:

How do I know that God is real? I have considered that question throughout my life, but it has come home that he is truly with me in recent, more difficult times.

In 2005 I was admitted to hospital for emergency surgery as a result of a twisted bowel. I have a vivid recollection, as I was given anaesthetics, of praying that God would look after me and bring me through the operation. My wife asked people in our own church to pray – and afterwards I was able to say that prayer made a difference and that God was real in a very obvious way, not least through the extraordinary feeling of peace which I experienced throughout.

I was told a twisted bowel could not happen again, but lightning did strike twice. The year 2007 brought a repeat performance in almost every respect, including God bringing me to a safe recovery in response to prayer, demonstrating his willingness to engage with his children.

Then in 2009 I was diagnosed with myeloma, a cancer affecting blood-cell production in the bone marrow. What had I done to deserve yet another health crisis? I could see many others experiencing severe problems and wondered about them too.

I spent an initial few days in hospital having the condition treated and various tests performed. Many prayed and I responded well. Weeks of treatment followed. I struggled at times as a result of its effects but the skills of expert medical staff, my determination to return to my normal life, the support of friends and family, our faith looking to God for healing – all these combined and I am now in full remission, not cured but restored to serve.

We cannot expect God to protect us from everything, but he is able to stand alongside, give us the courage to cope and, in my case, to recover from adversity. I read a piece in my daily Bible notes not long ago that underlined how in recent times I have drawn great personal strength from knowing that God is real:

> Faith must stand to the end, not give up at the last moment. Faith is not demonstrated through a trust in God in the good times; it is only in the extremities that faith is really

seen. This is not so that God will find out the strength of our faith, but so that we will know its strength.

(Dr John Wilks writing in *Encounter
With God*, Scripture Union, 2009)

Why is it that good people like Martin sometimes suffer so many bad things? Not an easy question to answer, though long books attempting to do so have been written by learned theologians. Normally they conclude that our world, which God pronounced 'good' when he made it, became corrupted as human beings kept rebelling against him. Death, decay, pain, sorrow all gained a foothold. Although God is outworking a plan for redeeming all of that, it hasn't yet come to its triumphant conclusion.

Here, though, I want to look at the question from the point of view of relationship. Suppose you know that God loves you. You're relating to him well, serving him, and then – wham, bang – troubles come along as thick and fast as if you'd suddenly found yourself in a war zone. They threaten to knock you for six.

The truth is that you *are* in a war zone. But God doesn't leave you there unequipped. You can choose to give up – but first take into account that there is effective armour and a battle plan for you. Paul, who knew all about being shipwrecked, beaten, imprisoned, ill, betrayed, misunderstood and so on, wrote this in his letter to the church in Ephesus:

> Put on the full armour of God, so that when the day of evil comes, you may be able to stand your ground, and after you have done everything, to stand. Stand firm then, with the belt of truth buckled round your waist, with the breastplate of righteousness in place, and with your feet fitted with the readiness that comes from the gospel of peace. In addition to all this, take up the shield of faith, with which you can extinguish all the flaming arrows of the evil one. Take the helmet of salvation and

the sword of the Spirit, which is the word of God. And pray in
the Spirit on all occasions with all kinds of prayers and requests.
With this in mind, be alert and always keep on praying for all
the saints. (Ephesians 6.13–18)

Lord, thank you that you heard and answered prayers for Martin,
even though the way was through, not straight out of, all those
pain-filled battles. Help us to keep praying for people we know
who are facing such battalions of troubles that they feel they
are in a war zone right now. And help us, when troubles come,
to be able to stand 'to the end' and face them, wearing your
special 'armour' – so that afterwards, whether we live on this
earth or die, we may be able to say in truth that our relationship with you is stronger than ever.

Does 'no help' mean God doesn't care – or lacks the power?

As [Jesus] approached the town gate, a dead person was being
carried out – the only son of his mother, and she was a widow.
And a large crowd from the town was with her. When the Lord
saw her, his heart went out to her and he said, 'Don't cry.'

Then he went up and touched the coffin, and those carrying
it stood still. He said, 'Young man, I say to you, get up!'

The dead man sat up and began to talk, and Jesus gave him
back to his mother. They were all filled with awe and praised
God. 'A great prophet has appeared among us,' they said. 'God
has come to help his people.' (Luke 7.12–16)

It's great following someone who has unlimited authority
and compassion. Those who meet him get healed – even raised
from the dead if necessary – and live happily ever after . . . except
it doesn't always work like that. I've prayed for people to
be healed. Some have been; others have gone on suffering,
or died. Why? Because Jesus lacks authority now? Because he

doesn't care about those people? Because he's not 'for real', he's like some cynical politician, never doing the good he's promised? No!

After Jesus disrupted that funeral we read of him assuring his cousin and 'forerunner', John (the Baptist), that all the healings and miracles were evidence that he, Jesus, was God's chosen one. He ends by saying, 'Blessed is the man who does not fall away on account of me.' Those whom Jesus had healed or raised from the dead falling away because of him? Whatever did he mean? He knew John was in prison (see Luke 3.20), likely to be put to death, and that he himself might well suffer a similar fate. Jesus never promised that following him would provide heavenly protection from all ills, but it is true that nothing can kill a loving relationship with his Father, God – not even sickness or death. We may know God as a distant, beneficent authority and be grateful for the good things he provides. But proving him trustworthy in our darkest experiences takes our relationship to a much deeper level.

Gayle Scott writes of such a time:

We'd spent the day laughing mostly; the morning was a little church get-together in my flat, followed by a friend's baby-shower and then a meal out at Nando's in Putney. Who'd have thought a day like that could end so brutally? I dropped my Ethiopian friend off outside her shabby block of flats; she climbed out of the squashed mini, doubled up with laughter at some joke. We said 'bye, she crossed the road and that was the last time I saw her. She was only 29.

I never thought of myself as a superstitious person, in fact I'd usually walk directly under ladders to prove a point. A good faith-filled Christian, I had no fear, trusting God instead. That night changed everything.

You see, that night my friend went home, watched some telly and then was knifed to death by her brother. He – a new Christian and a friend of mine too – was living with, struggling with, and that night momentarily defeated by, schizophrenia.

The next day I yanked God out of the middle of me and stood looking at him anew, concluding, 'I don't know you at all.' I had never felt such pain, such loss. And worse, penetrating the shock and the grief, outright disappointment, maybe even disgust, at this God I had always trusted.

Finally, about three months later, I realized I'd been sold a Christian lie. I'd been living with a so-called-faith concept which was really a kind of superstition – that, with God, bad things can't happen. It hit me like a brick one day while listening to that awesome Celtic band, 'Iona'. Their words captured the actions of monks who'd get in a boat and let the sea take them wherever, in order to share the good news about Jesus with those they might find. The song quotes from Psalm 139: 'If I make my bed in the depths, you are there . . . if I settle on the far side of the sea, even there your . . . right hand will hold me fast' – because God has been before us to all of these dark and distant places.

Hang on, I thought, they're saying that even if they drown they'll be surrounded by God's love. With my previous faith-superstition the concept that God might let me, or any faith-filled Christian, drown was offensive. However, now I think true faith involves saying that I will follow you God and, even if the worst does happen, your love will still surround me.

When her close Ethiopian friend was murdered, Gayle was living, school-teaching and serving God in a tough area of London. Not long afterwards, she moved to Inverness where her teaching qualifications weren't recognized – but because she believed God wanted her there she prayed, and, well past the eleventh hour at the start of the school year, was given leave to teach the toughest class in the place. She is one tiny woman but that class didn't know what had hit it. They saw miracles of physical and emotional healing, a few came to know God for themselves and together they became the most-improved, almost the best class, instead of the worst. Meanwhile Gayle, though very content being single, found herself thinking about marriage. It's a long story, but the man, quite literally, of her dreams, who was living near London 'found' her out of the blue in Inverness. A few years previously, his first wife had died of cancer despite fervent, worldwide volleys of prayer. Today Gayle and he are married, living happily in Mallorca and still on a sometimes knuckle-whitening adventure of faith with their God.

Lord, help us to know you in such a way that whatever happens, wherever we might end up and whatever unanswered questions we might have, you will have been there before us. You will remain our help, saviour and closest friend in whom we can confide, because you are totally for real and because you, amazingly, trust us.

Changing

The famous Lloyd Webber song says, 'Love changes everything' – and romantic love can do that, sometimes. God's love is far greater, though; it's perfect and his presence really does change everything – especially as we learn, a little at a time, to think, feel and act as he does. We don't have to be perfect to find his help; we merely have to acknowledge that we are needy, even broken – and ask him for it.

A bit at a time

> 'My thoughts are not your thoughts, neither are your ways my ways,' declares the LORD. 'As the heavens are higher than the earth, so are my ways higher than your ways and my thoughts than your thoughts.' (Isaiah 55.8–9)

This relationship between God Almighty and us as human beings poses a problem. As these ancient words say, God's thoughts and ways are so very different, so much 'higher' than ours. Surely expecting a relationship with such a being is as absurd as an ant expecting a relationship with you or me? Yet stories throughout the Bible are about God reaching out to us humans, offering real relationship with each individual – and with communities. And between two and three billion Christians in our world today would say they experience something of that extraordinary life-changing relationship with him.

So can our thoughts and ways change to be more like God's? One thing is for sure, we can't do it on our own. We need to be in that relationship to access his help, his strength, his

73

resources. That's because God's not into brainwashing or creating clone-slaves: he forms relationships more like those within a family. He wants us to co-operate with him.

God's presence is with Christians all the time but a myriad other sounds can distract our attention. When we acknowledge – or 'tune in' to – his presence, we start to see things differently, even to think and behave differently. Acknowledging that we trust him in the midst of painful, challenging or pleasant circumstances confirms that our side of the relationship with him is real and we find his promises concerning his relationship with us real too.

Steve Elmes, one of the ministers at my church, told us in a sermon about one way in which he has learnt to work this out practically.

Steve's days are busy with lots of different meetings, interspersed with informal conversations, complex pastoral problems, administration, decision-making, sermon preparation . . . not to mention vital time with his wife and three children. Rushing from one thing to another, he felt his relationship with God slipping. So he started to pray about how he could live in the Lord's presence, giving every thought, action and feeling over to him.

It seemed an impossibly big challenge but the answer came: 'Take it a little bit at a time.' Steve began with the 'transition times' in his day. Between meetings and other activities, he takes a moment to stop and say these simple words: 'Lord, you are here. Your presence fills this place. In your presence is peace, joy, love, courage . . .' (or whatever is appropriate). 'In all I have to do, I give myself to you.'

My life, like so many people's, is spent rushing from one thing to another, trying to keep all the different 'plates' spinning. The week after hearing Steve's sermon, a family emergency had me in a prolonged state of panic. I had no idea what to do for the best – but eventually recognizing God's presence and asking for his help eased my stress levels. It put a different complexion on the circumstances whenever I stopped and acknowledged, out loud, or in my head: 'Lord, you are here. Your presence fills this place. In your presence is peace, joy, love. In all I have to do, I give myself to you.'

God's presence melts right through anger, pain and exhaustion and lends a God's eye view. I knew that God was indeed there and would help – with my own attitude if nothing else.

Here's an invitation to receive help from God. It comes from earlier in the same chapter of Isaiah:

'Come, all you who are thirsty, come to the waters; and you who have no money, come, buy and eat! Come, buy wine and milk without money and without cost. Why spend money on what is not bread, and your labour on what does not satisfy? Listen, listen to me, and eat what is good, and your soul will delight in the richest of fare.

Give ear and come to me; hear me, that your soul may live. I will make an everlasting covenant with you, my faithful love promised . . . Seek the LORD while he may be found; call on him while he is near. Let the wicked forsake his way and the evil man his thoughts. Let him turn to the LORD, and he will have mercy on him, and to our God, for he will freely pardon.'

(Isaiah 55.1–3, 6–7)

Disappearing fears

Kathy Butler, a retired teacher from Dorset, writes of how Dan Dare changed her life:

When I was six, my big brother's favourite programme was *Dan Dare* on Radio Luxembourg. Sitting at the dining table, enjoying my mother's chunky soup for supper, we listened to exciting tales of rockets and space ships. One was about a red moon which came too close to earth, upsetting the days and seasons. I could see it so vividly in my mind. Was it actually happening? I began to wake at night wondering if it were really daytime but daylight had not come. I worried all winter that spring would never return.

Why didn't I tell my parents? I thought they would say I was silly – but to me, at the time, my fears were all too real.

After many months, in desperation I turned to the Bible I'd been given, hoping God could help. In bed that night I started at 'In the beginning'. In the book of Genesis I read about Adam and Eve, Cain and Abel. Then I came to the story of Noah and the flood. I scanned each page avidly for a message. When I reached Genesis chapter 8, verse 22 (AV), I discovered these wonderful words, 'While the earth remaineth, seedtime and harvest, and cold and heat, and summer and winter, and day and night shall not cease.' My relief was tremendous. God had spoken to me. What's more, he hadn't laughed at me for being silly. He'd been a gentleman, replying with a clear statement that I could understand and that allayed my very specific fears. Reassured immediately, every time I see a rainbow I still say a silent 'thank you' to God for his graciousness to a timid little girl.

I'm sure most of us can relate to Kathy's tale of an overpowering childhood fear which now, to us as adults, seems groundless. Yet adults too can open ourselves to fear, as Kathy did, by believing things which aren't true – for example, that an angry and eagle-eyed God is out to get us. So maybe, as with Kathy's story, it's time for a bit of truth. Jesus said, 'You will know the truth, and the truth will set you free' (John 8.32). God isn't watching in disapproval, ready to whack us with a big stick. Kathy wrote of her first experience of God speaking to her, and he's reaching out to each one of us too, yearning for us to experience his love, his comfort, his grace. He longs to calm our fears and that happens as we begin to know him and so to trust in him. The Bible says 'Don't be afraid' around the same number of times as there are days in the year. It also says that God is love, perfect love, which drives out fear. Makes sense: for the love of their children, parents will face any fear, from a sheer cliff-drop to the dragon of a headteacher. Even when our fears are completely rational, God is far bigger and more powerful than all of them!

God, our loving Father, welcomes us into his family – a community whose members are also learning that love, faith and trust are far greater than any fear. It doesn't happen overnight. We don't float through frightening situations on cloud nine, we have to turn to him and ask for help – but each time a fear is overcome we learn to trust him a little more.

Jesus' friend John wrote:

> We know and rely on the love God has for us. God is love. Whoever lives in love lives in God, and God in him ...
>
> There is no fear in love. But perfect love drives out fear, because fear has to do with punishment. The one who fears is not made perfect in love.
>
> We love because he first loved us.
>
> If anyone says, 'I love God,' yet hates his brother, he is a liar. For anyone who does not love his brother, whom he has seen, cannot love God, whom he has not seen.   (1 John 4.16–20)

Transformed!

Our son left home following some mid-teen years which made Harry Enfield's Kevin the Teenager look mild. To take one small aspect, his bedroom ... no, I won't describe it lest you are reading this while eating. Eight years later he returned to a newly carpeted and furnished room, for 14 relationship-renewing months. In the realm of attitude, helpfulness and behaviour, things were so much better in his late 20s than in his teens. The improvement in his bedroom was less marked, despite our laying down some ground rules. I did pray for him, especially that he would end up with a good woman. Now he has done so. They love each other and she has transformed him. Their tiny flat is astonishing – everything in its place and looking wonderful. She and her parents say that our son has been good for her too. They are 'right' as a couple because they draw the best out of each other. Think for a moment: how have relationships changed you, for good or ill?

Stories of people changing for the better because of their relationship with God fill the Bible – but, on first becoming a Christian, no one changes his or her whole character to become exactly like him. It takes time. A few call themselves Christians but never change. Jesus said, 'Do people pick grapes from thornbushes, or figs from thistles?' (Matthew 7.16). In other words, as we recognize a tree by its fruit, so, over time, we can tell whether people are really following him, by their attitudes and behaviour. God doesn't change. He certainly doesn't change to become like us – selfish, spiteful, unreliable, dishonest and so on. Instead, his pure, consistent and powerful love makes all the difference to us, if we let it.

Take the story of rough, tough fisherman Simon in the Bible. Jesus chose him as one of his closest friends, changed his name to Peter (meaning 'Rock' in Greek) and pronounced him a firm foundation for the faith community he was building. Why Simon Peter? Unreliable, impetuous, argumentative, lying, bragging-brave but in the event cowardly, uneducated, uncouth Simon Peter! In three years of closeness with Jesus, the guy couldn't grasp any more than the rest of them what Jesus was trying to do – apart from that one astonishing statement, 'You are the Christ, the Son of the living God' (Matthew 16.16).

Jesus saw something in Simon Peter that I wouldn't have seen. After Jesus ascended into heaven, the Holy Spirit drew out his rock-like qualities. I find it so encouraging that Simon Peter became a bold and great missionary. The changes in his attitudes and behaviour didn't stop there. For example, Acts 10 tells how he thought Jesus' message was only for the Jews until the Holy Spirit gave him a vision. Then he changed his belief and attitude straightaway and obeyed God by taking his message to Gentiles also.

Pauline from Wales tells the story of how change happened within her own marriage:

It began OK. I was a Christian when I met Mark. He was sympathetic enough to pray inwardly and come along to church with me. The real problems kicked off as we started our family. I'd been the main breadwinner but, after becoming pregnant, couldn't return to work. A builder by trade, Mark is a simple man of humble requirements. He never intended to run his own business, but now the pressure to pay the bills and build a future for our family rested squarely on his shoulders.

Watching Mark run his own business has been like watching a suspense movie while sitting on a rollercoaster on a rainy day – very unpredictable. Alcohol became a route he took to comfort himself in his many stresses. He sensed that his life was out of control. No matter what he tried, he felt a failure – to himself, to me and to our children.

I have prayed for him through all of our 19 years together. The stronger his desperation, the more I prayed and the harder he fought God. He said he wanted what I had and was asking God for it, but wasn't receiving.

I was given a vision a few years ago, while praying for Mark. God told me that he wanted to bring this man to his knees. Sometimes we need to be brought to our knees so that God can raise us up and help us. A few days later, Mark nearly lost a leg from a knee infection caused by a sliver of concrete. He recovered, but still had no living relationship with Jesus. Through a chronic back problem, still he fought, for almost two years.

My miscarriage made him angrier. The word 'divorce' was thrown around.

Then something miraculous happened. On New Year's Eve, he made a pact with God. If he didn't receive a New Year's message from anyone, then he would give up alcohol for good. He received none and is now completely teetotal. That seemed to pave the way for what happened next.

One week after New Year I persuaded him to attend a gospel concert. There he gave his heart to Jesus. This big, strong, angry man had found peace at last. Through putting all his faith in the Lord he has found an incredible inner strength, often challenging my own faith. I see a wonderful future for our family, with God at the centre. Fear seems to have packed its bags and left us. In its place is peace, because we know that God loves us and will provide.

Willingness to change, to love and accommodate each other is vital in both parties for a good marriage relationship, yet we know it doesn't always happen that way. That's why we laugh at the old joke of the bride proclaiming: 'Aisle, altar, hymn!' She won't change him and, with that attitude, he won't change her! Yet God's power can help all of us to change in areas which have become 'stuck'.

Turning around

Cath Rathbone, a divorced mother of two, was born in Uruguay and also lived in the USA for 15 years before moving to England in October 2009. She writes:

'You're going to Texas to get sober,' he informed me on 19 January 2007, his voice loud and so clear that I whipped around to see who'd walked into the empty room. No one.

I laughed. My high-powered job was offering to move me from Florida to Texas. As a Christian of 21 years I'd been praying, asking God whether or not I should accept.

'Right. I'll go.' I laughed again. God's audible declaration was certainly unexpected, probably insane! As it turned out, it was I who was insane.

Arriving in Dallas on 15 April 2007 I discovered it was a dry county: no alcohol for sale! I shuddered, yet drove elsewhere to buy it. The pressure of my life and job were slowly killing me. To soothe it, I drank, not realizing how bad it had become.

That I knew no one in Dallas and made no attempt to meet anyone should have acted as another red flag but I found it suited me just fine. Once back from the office I could isolate in my flat and drink.

Until 28 May. Shaking, broken and dying, while on my knees at the foot of my bed, I wrote a 'prayer poem' in a drunken scrawl, begging God's help.

His forgiveness was instant, whispered into my heart, yet I had the audacity to negotiate. I was in sales, that's what I did.

'If that really is you, God, I'll only believe it if you get me a . . .', and I made a list of 12 conditions: a Christian counsellor – male, practising nearby, affordable rates, understood alcoholism, blah blah blah.

Another 'whisper' prompted me to my computer and I staggered over. Three mouse clicks and the 12 conditions were met!

I sobbed. I wept. I begged forgiveness for being so stubborn. It still took me a long time to recognize he'd forgiven me the moment I'd asked him on my knees at the foot of my bed.

Because that's who he is. His forgiveness is instant, unconditional, and wipes our slate clean. While I may insist on still carrying the shame of my past, he does not and he begs me to let it go too.

The journey through recovery hasn't been easy, but this gentle, patient God has been by my side every step of the way. I was made redundant three months after arriving in Texas, but that's a story for another day!

What a dramatic story – God even speaks to Cath with an audible voice! That's quite rare. When he helps me turn from harmful ways, thought-patterns and reactions towards his own good ways he's often more subtle. Here's one example:

I was so very angry. A woman of nearly 90 (not my mum) was going home to live alone after over a month in hospital, much of it spent immobile in bed. I and many others who cared had visited, made preparations, ensured that a care plan and various equipment were in place and talked the whole thing through with her, endlessly.

Then, when she came to be discharged, she refused all such help. We took her home, but after a couple of hours had to leave her in the house with someone else and go off to a meeting of people who lead worship in our church. We rushed in at the last minute and I exploded my anger all over them, leaving them in no uncertainty about how I was feeling – stressed, helpless, betrayed, exhausted, deeply worried . . . I went on and on about the unfairness of a system which won't hear reason but listens instead to a woman who thinks she can cope but quite obviously can't.

Finally, someone gave out song sheets and started to lead us in some quiet worship. There were only about ten of us there but these people loved God and, as they worshipped, his presence, his grace, filled the room. I started to weep, my anger and frustration dissolving and flowing away with my tears. I could do nothing more for the woman at present but I could trust God, let him carry all my negative feelings away and replace them with his comfort and peace. I prayed out loud to this effect, asking God's forgiveness, thanking him for it. I asked for his help to keep a better attitude in the future, as well in the outworking of the elderly woman's dilemma.

He kept his side of the bargain. When I've reneged on mine in similar circumstances since, giving way to destructive emotions, he's there, reminding me that he is trustworthy and that I can turn away from 'natural human' reactions such as anger and frustration. I can instead lean on him to find the love and the peace that I (and others involved) need.

If we claim that we experience a shared life with him and continue to stumble around in the dark, we're obviously lying through our teeth – we're not *living* what we claim ... On the other hand, if we admit our sins – make a clean breast of them – he won't let us down; he'll be true to himself. He'll forgive our sins and purge us of all wrongdoing.

(1 John 1.6–9 *The Message*)

If one of my small children hurt the other one, I would go on loving both but not rest until I'd made peace between them, no matter how loving and helpful the guilty one was towards me. Just so, God loves all his children; if we hurt each other he wants to sort it out. The ones responsible for doing the hurt need not only to say they are sorry to God, find his forgiveness and do the same with the people they've hurt. Even more important is to change their attitude and behaviour so it doesn't happen again.

Repentance isn't so much about feeling sorry or guilty as 'turning around' – something we find difficult. The good news is that God helps us, if we ask him. Any relationship with God doesn't play out in isolation. Any unloving thing that we do, say or think about ourselves or another person hurts God as well as that person. So how can he keep offering us forgiveness and a new start? Because when Jesus died, without sin, on a Roman gibbet and three days later his Father God raised him from the dead, the power of sin was broken. Jesus had taken its consequences upon himself. We can tap into all of that, for the asking. His forgiveness and his help to turn around is always available.

Forgiving others

The son of a friend of mine was killed at the age of 21. He and two girls were in a car driven by another young man, who was drunk after their night out. It turned out that he had neither driving licence nor insurance. The car slammed into a tree and caught fire. Its driver ran away. A man living in a nearby house, awoken by the noise of the crash, called the emergency services and even risked his own life getting the injured girls out. My friend's son never regained consciousness.

I saw my friend slog through weeks, months and years of what is known as 'the grieving process' – so painful, even to watch. Yet right from the start she said, 'I forgive the driver. I can't afford not to.' When the police found him they prosecuted. My friend travelled a long way to visit him in prison to tell him that she forgave him and wished him no harm. She saw him just that one time and didn't know if he appreciated it, or changed as a result. But, as she said, 'Grief is bad enough. I can't add to it by feelings of bitterness, or a consuming desire that he should suffer. That would only hurt me more.'

Forgiveness doesn't mean exonerating a person or explaining away the wrong he or she has done. It does involve, not revenge, but wanting the best for that person.

My friend had many questions to ask of God, but she didn't give up on her relationship with him because she knew that, more than anything or anyone else, he could help her through. Another reason for her to forgive was because she knew that God had forgiven her much. It had cost him the death of his own Son on the cross to exercise that forgiveness, illustrating how fundamental forgiveness is to him. A relationship where one party flouts something of fundamental importance to the other will flounder.

Rachel Kamara writes of a more 'everyday' issue of forgiveness which affected her own relationship with God for a while:

> I had just moved to a new flat and asked the housing manager to send the handyman to help me assemble some new furniture. The handyman did an excellent job, but on his return informed the housing manager that I had a satellite dish in my flat. The manager then wrote me a strongly worded letter, accusing me of violating management policy, which meant that I could have lost my home!
>
> I was most surprised as I'd never had a satellite dish – but then I thought of the round table which I'd folded flat and put behind my sofa. Could the handyman have seen and reported that as a satellite dish?
>
> Replying to the letter I explained – but decided I'd never again have anything to do with the handyman, even though the housing manager apologized on his behalf. It took a long time for me to get over it. Whenever I thought about that handyman I had no peace of mind – until the day I asked God to forgive me for holding a grudge. That moment brought much peace to me. I see the handyman often nowadays. I greet him nicely and know God has forgiven me.

Jesus told a story in response to a question about how many times we should forgive a person. You can read it in Matthew 18.21–35. A servant who owed his master thousands begged for time to pay – and his master cancelled his debt. Whereupon the servant seized another servant who owed him a few pence. He refused to allow the man time to pay and had him thrown into prison. When the master found out, he was furious and punished the first servant severely. Jesus said, 'This is how my heavenly Father will treat each of you unless you forgive your brother from your heart.'

There are times when our relationship with God doesn't appear to be 'for real'. He seems miles away, uncaring, hostile even. One reason could be because we're doing something wrong. Until we repent and give him a chance to forgive us, our relationship can't be restored. A specific case of this is when we refuse to forgive someone else. Jesus said, 'If you forgive men when they sin against you, your heavenly Father will also forgive you. But if you do not forgive men their sins, your Father will not forgive your sins' (Matthew 6.14–15). If I'm unforgiving towards someone, God is unlikely to be very 'real' to me. Forgiveness is far from easy but God will help, if we ask him.

Getting on

Jo Withers writes:

It might be another scorching day but still there is work to be done, I thought, as I swept the lifeless concrete floor. My thoughts kept churning. Two lives given over to God, two women feeling he'd called us to work here in a foreign land – how could we get on so badly? Was it the clash of cultures between the UK and the USA causing one or other of us to misconstrue almost every sentence – or something deeper? Was it me? My relationship with God had made so much sense previously but now . . . did it even exist? Was I really a Christian? The question horrified me.

The more I thought, the less sure I became but I kept my inner turmoil to myself for fear of further misunderstandings.

As the weeks passed and the days grew ever hotter, my sense of certainty diminished to a little pinprick: I must know God. Otherwise I wouldn't be here. With threads of certainty worn so thin, the Bible seemed full of endless empty words instead of life – until someone took time to show me the thread of life running through the whole story. It was like discovering building blocks for a solid foundation on which my life could be rebuilt: God's faithfulness from creation, to fall, to flood and exile. Then human kings and a baby born into poverty, who became a king executed on a tree that I might have life. That I might have life!

Now reading the Bible was no longer a dead academic exercise. Page after page revealed love – reigning, conquering, softening my heart and changing me from the inside out. Releasing this love and joy smoothed the rough edges of my life, exposing the darkness and allowing light into the secret places, the bits I never wanted to acknowledge, even to myself.

That oh-so-difficult relationship changed too. Not through words but through love and, as God opened my eyes to a different dimension, prayer. It never became easy, but now that American woman and I can relate in the light of God's love rather than in the darkness of our own minds.

If we're to follow a God who is pure love and Jesus who came to this earth as a servant – a giver par excellence without a selfish bone in his body – then it's clear that we'll have to change. Most of us may not go around hurting other people consciously but we're often self-centred and hesitate to love the unlovely. We serve others and give a bit but ... there are limits! Except there aren't, not with God. Which sounds a little harsh, as does the first part of Jo's story. She'd given up a lot to work hard for God in that hot country, only to find a difficult relationship upsetting everything, even her own faith. Jo simply couldn't find it in herself to get on with that American woman.

Jo needed to change, or rather to let God's love change her. What seemed like a horrible setback was in fact applied discipline which became a stepping stone for her to become a more loving and Christlike person.

Hebrews 12.10–11 (TLB) says:

Our earthly fathers trained us for a few brief years, doing the best for us that they knew how, but God's correction is always right and for our best good, that we may share his holiness.

Being punished isn't enjoyable while it is happening – it hurts! But afterwards we can see the result, a quiet growth in grace and character.

God doesn't set out to make our lives difficult but to make them better. Jesus said: 'The thief comes only to steal and kill and destroy; I have come that they may have life, and have it to the full' (John 10.10).

Communication, guidance

I watched our blind neighbour striding along behind his guide dog and marvelled at the communication and trust between them. Of course, it had to be learnt. Human beings and dogs are different species, they don't speak the same language. Nor do human beings and God, yet Christians insist that he really does communicate with and guide them.

How do humans and God communicate?

Jesus said: 'When you pray, go into your room, close the door and pray to your Father, who is unseen. Then your Father, who sees what is done in secret, will reward you. And when you pray, do not keep on babbling like pagans, for they think they will be heard because of their many words. Do not be like them, for your Father knows what you need before you ask him.'

(Matthew 6.6–8)

'Prayer' sounds like a special religious word – difficult territory to be tackled by spiritual giants only. Here Jesus is saying it doesn't need to be complicated because it's all about an intimate relationship. You couldn't have such a relationship without communication, though how on earth human beings can talk with or relate to God can appear a mystery at first. Yet he loves to hear us and for us to listen to him too. Our communication is unusual because our physical ears can't hear what he's saying and because he 'hears' us, no matter where we are, in whatever language we speak to him and whether we pray out loud or silently.

Individuals find different methods of communication with God helpful. Some find written, published prayers helpful – but special words for praying aren't necessary. Many use a structure like this: acknowledging God's greatness and presence first; saying sorry and asking forgiveness for anything they've done wrong since last time they prayed (setting the relationship right); then thanking God for specific things, and finally asking him for things, for others and for themselves. Some pour out their hearts, including the inconsequential affairs of the moment – much as I used to do to my longsuffering mother on arriving home after school most days – chatting away to God as though to their best friend. Some like to sit or kneel quietly in a special place, listening more than speaking; others pray while walking, doing routine chores or when they lie awake at night.

God knows our thoughts, so we don't need to speak out loud, though some do. Some pray at full volume when driving alone in the car – though if stuck in traffic with the windows open this may provoke strange looks from other drivers! Sometimes I find that writing my prayers down helps to focus my mind.

Although praying aloud with others present may feel difficult at first, I find it easier now than praying on my own – and Jesus promised to be wherever 'two or three come together in my name' (Matthew 18.20). Some don't use words at all but sit in a group, in silence, enjoying God's presence, making space to respond to him.

Most of us live such busy lives that we find it hard to still ourselves enough to listen properly with our 'spiritual ears' – but when we do, the rewards are great in terms of a deepened relationship with God, a sense of being loved, of reassurance or comfort. Sometimes that's 'all' it is. At other times we're stirred up and equipped to do a specific task – maybe to put something right or apologize to someone. We may be prompted to read a particular bit of the Bible through which God communicates in a way relevant to that moment. Some people sense God speaking words and may even write them down; others see an image in their mind's eye.

Veronica Heley, author of over 60 books and currently writing two gentle crime series, wrote this piece in response to my question, 'How do you know that God loves, forgives and accepts you?'

Sometimes when I pray, he puts a picture in my mind. Something I'd never have thought of for myself. For many years I've been a member of small prayer groups, most often consisting of just three people. Although I have a bad knee and can no longer kneel to pray, he gives me a comforting picture of three kneeling figures in the dark, who are praying. Streams of light arc from one to another and back again, doubling and redoubling all the time. Whenever I falter in prayer, I think of this and remember how powerful prayer can be when two or more are gathered together in his name.

Sometimes I hear his voice. He says to me, 'Veronica, do you love me?' I say, 'Yes, Lord; you know that I do.' In years gone by, he used to say, 'Feed my lambs,' and I'd know that my next book should be for children. Nowadays, he says, 'Feed my sheep,' which means I am to bring a Christian perspective into my crime stories. It is wonderful to have that confirmation that I'm on the right track in my work.

I suffer times of stress, like anyone else. Recently I've found that I can kneel (in my head) before him, and hand him a tangled ball made up of all my problems and fears. He doesn't give me back a nicely wound up ball of wool. No. He floats out before me a piece of fine material; sometimes blue and sometimes golden. Sometimes it has a random spread of real flowers on it; sometimes it's plain. I can wrap myself in this, I can use it as a cloak. It makes me laugh out loud to see how much he cares for me, and how he lets me know it.

Lord, help me not to worry about praying but simply to get on and do it, believing that you hear me when I talk to you and that you are longing to communicate with me too. Help me to listen so that we can have proper conversations and I can get to know you better, amazing as that might sound.

Communication – our speaking

In order to grow and flourish, any relationship needs good communication. So let's consider a little more how we might speak to God. I asked a couple of people, who are a lot better than I am at praying, how they do it.

Rachel Kamara, originally from Sierra Leone, now settled in West London, told me that she prays throughout the day:

> We don't always need to talk, not with words, anyway. The Bible says, 'the Spirit helps us in our weakness. We do not know what we ought to pray for, but the Spirit himself intercedes for us with groans that words cannot express' (Romans 8.26). When I set aside a special time to talk to him I structure it in the order you see in the Lord's prayer. I start by acknowledging who he is in praise and adoration: 'Our Father in heaven, may your name be held holy,' then go on to his agenda: 'Your kingdom come, your will be done on earth as it is in heaven.' I pray for others' needs as well as my own: 'Give us this day our daily bread.' I ask for forgiveness, for right relationship with him and with other people – and that God will keep us all on the right path: 'And forgive us our sins as we forgive those who sin against us. And lead us not into temptation but deliver us from evil.' So I always put thankfulness and praise first. I wouldn't just rush up to a friend demanding something, except in an emergency! I'd greet the friend, kiss her perhaps, ask how she is, put her agenda first – and it's similar with God. I keep an ever-growing list of people I'm praying for, sometimes more spring to mind – but I pray for others before I pray for myself.

Annemarie Aurmoogum also prays 'all the time', while she goes about her busy life:

> Doing shift work in the caring professions, it's the only way. Expressing simple thankfulness to him for little things has become a habit. Sometimes I'm silent and focus on the Lord. Sometimes I use the words of a song or hymn to worship him, or read a psalm or other passage in the Bible. I know people who dance or clap as they pray.
>
> If bad things happen, even though I may not understand, I tell God that I trust him. I ask him to help me, to give me his peace and to let me see clearly what I should do. We can't change people – but God can, so I believe it's important to pray for them, especially if they're not getting on well with each other. If someone is too ill to pray I suggest they hold on to a cross in their hand – because Jesus dying on the cross and rising again is at the basis of our faith. And then I pray very simply for them, to their creator and saviour.

Anne Reid tells a story where off-the-cuff conversations with God have unexpected outcomes:

> The tickets were like gold dust. I felt like Charlie with his Golden Ticket to the famed chocolate factory – but mine was to a weekend's Christian conference in Wembley Stadium.
>
> My suitcase, well packed, stood at the back of my school classroom in London. As I taught the class I counted down the hours. And then I heard the voice in my ear. 'You are to go to Lowestoft tonight.'
>
> I was stupefied. 'Lowestoft? No, I'm going to Wembley!'
>
> As I continued trying to teach the children I kept hearing the same message. An audible voice to me, the children couldn't hear it and must have wondered why their teacher was so distracted and kept muttering to herself.
>
> 'No, I'm going to Wembley. You know how hard it was to get that ticket!'

I thought about Lowestoft – a Suffolk town lying 100 miles in the opposite direction from Wembley. A few years previously I'd spent four years in a convent there, trying to become a nun. I'd some fond memories, including of Sister Mary, whom I loved very much. Mary had left her native Ireland at 15 to enter the order, along with her two sisters, sent by their father to escape poverty at home. Now in her mid-eighties, Mary had given years of service in the convent boarding school's refectory, kitchen and laundry, but somehow her intellectual abilities had never been encouraged. She'd withdrawn into herself, hiding both her disappointment and her great sense of humour.

By now I was at Marylebone Station, all geared up to go to Wembley, while God was still instructing me to go to Lowestoft. Having spent some time informing him, angrily, that he had it all wrong, I caught a train to Lowestoft, arriving well after most of the elderly sisters were in bed. I rang the huge bell and waited in apprehension. How would they react to my arriving unannounced and uninvited? Mother Superior opened the door and peered cautiously out into the darkness.

'Oh, thanks be to God, you've come!' she exclaimed. 'We've all been praying so hard that you would. Mary's in a dreadful state. She's going to the psychiatric hospital on Monday.' She told me that Mary had locked herself in her room, refusing to come out or to let anyone in. 'We imagine the room is in quite a state,' she warned me, before I banged on its door.

When I yelled back at Mary's protestations she was so surprised to recognize my voice that she let me in. She showed me a huge book in which she'd written all her anger and pain at not being given the chance to use her intellect, when other sisters had trained as teachers, nurses or social workers. 'I'm sending this to Mother General!'

Mother General was boss of the whole order. I asked if I might read the book first. After a few pages I was weeping.

She asked if we should post the book to Mother General.

'We could – but I know someone who would take better care of your pain and sorrow.'

Page by page we handed all the anger and sadness over to Jesus – and then we went out in the back garden to burn all that pain (not the normal convent routine!). Mary's whole body looked lighter, her eyes shone with love and peace and we danced an undignified, joyful war-dance as the book disappeared into smoke.

Mary said, 'And now for some supper!' She returned to her room, washed and changed out of her filthy clothes. She remained in her right mind for the four years until a heart attack ended her life, so she never occupied that bed in the psychiatric hospital. Her last words were, 'Be still and know that I am God.'

Thank God that he knows best and that I went to Lowestoft, not to the Christian healing conference at Wembley that weekend!

We learn by experience that God hears us – and replies. You'll find many examples in this book of his answers to people's very specific prayers. You can find the Lord's Prayer in Matthew 6.9–15 and Luke 11.2–4. Why not use its 'headlines' as Rachel does and then go on talking to God about your day, your worries, those you're concerned about?

Communication – our listening

Unlike Anne I've never heard God's voice with my ears, the way I would with a human being. Sometimes he highlights words I'm reading in the Bible, or an object, event, something said . . . He might give me an impression, a picture in my mind's eye, a single word or phrase. He conveys many things without needing words, let alone a voice, and I'm surprised how often he uses humour. Recently I was stressed in the kitchen, racing to get everything served up on time. The words 'You're not on *Ready, Steady, Cook*' popped into my mind – and as I laughed

I understood that God meant my lifestyle as well as my culinary disasters. Slow down Chris, life's not a race!

Everyone is different, so I asked some others how God communicates with them.

Rachel Kamara said: 'First thing in the morning I'm often silent. I listen. I might get a little prompt to go and see a particular person. How do I know that "thought" comes from God? When it comes not once but several times.'

Young mother Juliette Lambert said: 'God can communicate in so many different ways – for example I have experienced his presence and blessing through smell. On the day we finally moved into our new house I was struck by a very strong smell of incense as I entered it – God's way of telling me what a blessing this house would be.'

Cath Rathbone writes:

> In 2001, when I was newly divorced, our rector taught us a writing-meditation exercise for listening to God. In a quiet place, with a sheet of paper or a journal, invite God into a conversation. First, write down what's happening around you: cars, noises, moving objects and such, so you can let them go. Then listen and begin to write. Write everything you hear. Don't select. Don't judge. Just write. I'm dyslexic and normally have to rewrite, edit, and correct constantly. Yet when God speaks and I write his words there are never any errors, cross outs or corrections. I'm amazed. The calm voice which I hear in my inner ear never races around like my own thoughts. God is always patient as I write in longhand and never loses his train of thought. That's my experience – others' will be different, I'm sure.

Jennifer Louis, a gardening grandmother from Dorking, writes about how she learnt to listen better to the voice of Jesus:

> I've trusted Jesus for years. The more I've asked him for help, the more he has given. My life has ticked along nicely. I'm cheerful, exuberant, busy, always on the lookout for self-improvement.

And then I became ill. Had to return home from looking after a family in deepest Siberia, live on my own and rest. That wasn't so easy! What was God saying to me now? What did he want me to do?

One day I was rereading an article by a good friend who suggested it was not civilized to eat in front of the telly. I decided to take that simple improvement on board. I carried my tray to the table, set my untouched lunch out properly and sat down. Alone in the unaccustomed silence I felt slight withdrawal symptoms, as we do when the computer goes down. Feeling both anxious and impatient, I asked, 'So what am I supposed to be doing now?'

The answer came back straightaway. 'I've been waiting for you!'

Wow! My first reaction was laughter. Could it really be that simple and obvious? Moses had to go up a mountain but here was God speaking to me in my own familiar dining-room.

God had been longing for my undivided attention – all my life, I suppose. Once I'd made a space in my day and started the conversation myself, there he was, as close, loving, gentle and patient as could be!

Those few words, that communication, turned my life around. I realized that I'd been much too busy and talkative. I'd also been unappreciative. I needed to become calmer and keep my diary much less full. Even though my illness had slowed me down, I recognized tendencies to be off again at the first opportunity, faster and faster, like the Red Queen.

I've changed. I've learnt to listen. For example, I've learnt to regard waking at night as God's gift of a special listening time. My relationship with him has grown so much!

How do we know it is God speaking to us, not our imagination or wishful thinking? Jesus explained it in terms of sheep, which in his time would all be kept safe, mixed up with other flocks in the village fold at night. Each sheep would come to know and trust its own shepherd who led it to good pasture and looked after it by day. Shepherds don't speak sheep language, nor are sheep renowned for their intelligence, yet every morning each sheep recognized its own shepherd's voice among the rest, listened and followed him because they had, within sheep limits, a real relationship with him. This is what Jesus said:

> The man who enters by the gate is the shepherd of his sheep. The watchman opens the gate for him, and the sheep listen to his voice. He calls his own sheep by name and leads them out. When he has brought out all his own, he goes on ahead of them, and his sheep follow him because they know his voice. But they will never follow a stranger; in fact, they will run away from him because they do not recognize a stranger's voice . . . I am the good shepherd; I know my sheep and my sheep know me – just as the Father knows me and I know the Father – and I lay down my life for the sheep. I have other sheep that are not of this sheep pen. I must bring them also. They too will listen to my voice, and there shall be one flock and one shepherd.
>
> (John 10.2–5, 14–16)

Can you make time and space to listen to him today?

This way!

Maybe one of our most fundamental needs as human beings is to know why we're here and what we're meant to be doing with our lives. God gives us that sense of direction and purpose but doesn't always paint it clear in big letters across our skies. Jo Withers writes of the process God took her through:

> The direction that I was heading was without question: Southern Sudan. Once the paperwork had come through I could begin sorting my financial support, along with everything else necessary to move abroad for at least four years. Not a daunting prospect – I'd done it before – though every time is slightly

different. This time the wheels were grinding unbearably slowly. By January it felt like I had been waiting for ever.

Mustering as much patience as I could, I decided that for one week I would try not to think about the future. Instead I would enjoy a time of rest and refreshment in one of the most beautiful places on this earth.

Apart from one teenager, I was the youngest at this Christian conference centre by over 20 years, but was too tired to bother about that. My life in Africa sparked much interest and questions from other guests. I found the atmosphere a little too intense for my liking. I tried to sit through talks but, with a brain like jelly and my body tense, failed to take anything in. Instead I escaped into the wonders of God's amazing creation, so present and intimate. Not even I could fail to see God in this place – the robin that came and perched on the tip of my walking boot for what seemed like eternity became a real sign that he was near.

As the week continued, and I was asked time and again about my future plans, my voice seemed ever more detached from my mind and body. My sincerity evaporated and, though I continued to talk about wanting the Sudan to be the next step on my journey, I'd become less and less convinced.

'But God,' I cried, 'what else? Surely this is it. Don't ask me not to return to Africa!'

During the final meal of the week a man who had prayed for me earlier that day said, 'If everything else goes pear-shaped, you should think about joining this community.' (The place is run by a 90-strong international community of Christians who live and work there.)

Outwardly polite, I thought, yeh, right, I know what I'm going to do and it doesn't involve working here. But, however hard I tried to convince myself, the seed-thought was planted. During the final service of the week it wouldn't leave my mind but grew until I knew what I had to do – at least apply to join the Christian community.

A few weeks later, back for an interview, it was like Cinderella's slipper fitting perfectly. I felt so at home – no need to keep pushing against slowly grinding wheels. Taking a few moments out, I climbed high up on a hill close to three large wooden crosses looking out over the sea. There I sat, watching the birds soaring effortlessly, thinking about the learning curve of fledglings beginning to fly. Starting with small distances close to the safety of the rocks and their mother, they strengthen their wings, travel further, become more daring, until they hardly have to think about where their next stopping point will be. I cried to God, 'Teach me to fly; I want to fly with the birds!'

Fifteen months on, the flying lessons continue. My wings are growing stronger, the distances I am able to fly longer and my flight patterns less erratic. I am now less dependent on knowing where the next resting place is going to be, yet there is still much learning to do.

Sometimes I try in vain to imagine what my life would have been like had I headed to Southern Sudan. I do know that I am in a much better place now to consider such a transition. In bringing me here, God knew what he was doing – exactly what I needed. Looking back, I can see that it was not the mission agency that was causing the wheels to grind so slowly, it was God. He knew that the Sudan was not right for me at that time and his job was to get that through to me! As I walk in the rugged beauty of this place I remember the robin and how God met me here. I am so thankful that he continues to meet me when I need it most.

In a close relationship with another human being, we share our hopes and dreams, our fears and frustrations. We value the other person's wisdom and input since that person knows us better than we know ourselves. When we're unsure about something, we ask their advice, or go through the pros and cons together. But how can we do all that with God? We can't hear his voice (normally) and yet Christians say they converse with him, listen to him – that he guides them through difficult decisions, through the whole of life.

Jo's story illustrates how this can work. She says she can see how he did it when she looks back – and that is often the way. He spoke to her through another person – one who had been praying for her. He guided through circumstances – the extra-long delays in paperwork. He spoke as she relaxed and enjoyed the natural world's beauty, enabling her to see a bigger picture, in particular through birds. He spoke through what felt 'right'. He knew her better than she knew herself. For one with a (normally) inaudible voice, he's very good at getting his message across! Our part is to trust him, expecting that he will communicate with us and guide us in the direction that we need to go.

Seven hundred years before Jesus, the prophet Isaiah wrote these words: 'Whether you turn to the right or to the left, your ears will hear a voice behind you, saying, "This is the way; walk in it"' (Isaiah 30.21).

Dreams and visions

'These men are not drunk, as you suppose. It's only nine in the morning! No, this is what was spoken by the prophet Joel: '"In the last days, God says, I will pour out my Spirit on all people. Your sons and daughters will prophesy, your young men will see visions, your old men will dream dreams. Even on my servants, both men and women, I will pour out my Spirit in those days, and they will prophesy."'

(Acts 2.15–18, quoting from Joel 2.28–29)

After Jesus died and was raised from the dead, he appeared to his frightened little band of followers and told them to wait in Jerusalem until the Holy Spirit came to empower them. The words quoted above are his friend Simon Peter's explanation to a bewildered crowd from many nations who had assembled in the Holy City for the Jewish harvest festival. Suddenly this small group of men and women, most of them 'country bumpkins' from the outlying province of Galilee, were speaking all kinds of other languages, 'as the Spirit enabled them'.

'Drunk' seems an odd diagnosis for people suddenly fluent in languages unknown to them previously. But Jesus' friends had just met the third person of the Trinity – the Holy Spirit – a powerful and overwhelmingly joyful experience. He comes to live within us, closer than Jesus or the Father, closer than breathing – and yet he is supernatural God! We're not drunk – but inexplicable things do happen.

Wiebke, who comes from Germany, lived in my village with her English husband Edward Smith for many years. Sensible, level-headed and a much-respected member of the community, Wiebke was a licensed lay minister at our parish church, loved for her pastoral work and preaching. She led a cross-church team that takes assemblies in almost all the local schools. She told me how a dream which God gave her as a young woman had changed her life. Clearly, dreams are not the sole province of old men – a supernatural God communicates with us in all kinds of surprising ways! Wiebke writes:

It was July 1963 when I travelled with a German girl friend from our home in Hamburg to Lee Abbey, a Christian conference and holiday centre in North Devon. There we attended an 'Overseas Houseparty', which lasted a fortnight.

A different houseparty had ended on the day we arrived. One of its guests, by the name of Edward Smith, had just found out he could no longer visit family friends in another part of Devon, as he'd planned, and asked if he could stay on at Lee Abbey for a few days. He spoke briefly to me while we both helped with the washing up. Realizing that I was at a loose end, as my German friend had fallen ill, Edward invited me and two Danish girls for a trip to Coombe Martin in his Morris Minor.

Four days later, when Edward left Lee Abbey, we exchanged addresses and he offered to show me around London, should I ever decide to go there.

Back in Hamburg in October 1963, I had a vivid dream, the kind you remember when you wake. Edward was sitting next to me as we sped through Great Britain on an endless train journey. We said not a word but I felt so secure and happy. Thinking about that dream afterwards I assumed it meant that I would settle down to live in England. Then a letter arrived from Edward, with photos of me and the two Danish girls at Coombe Martin.

Shortly after Christmas I went to stay for a few days with Edward and his parents in their home in Twickenham. He took me around some of the London sights and to a few concerts.

Then, at Easter 1964, Edward travelled to Hamburg to stay with my parents. We became engaged, fixing our wedding for 25 July. Between our first encounter and our wedding day we saw each other for a total of only four weeks. I'd never have risked uprooting myself to live in another country with Edward were it not for that God-given dream. But, as I write in July 2009, the 'train journey' has lasted for a very happy 45 years!

I am forever grateful to God for assuring me that England was the country and Edward the man for me.

I believe God had work for Wiebke to do here too! He's only too willing to show us what he wants us to do. Jesus said: 'Ask and it will be given to you; seek and you will find; knock and the door will be opened to you.'

He also said that if we want the Holy Spirit to be closer to us than breathing, he himself is longing for us to ask, because he longs to give. Jesus said: 'Which of you fathers, if your son asks for . . . an egg, will give him a scorpion? If you . . . know how to give good gifts to your children, how much more will your Father in heaven give the Holy Spirit to those who ask him!' (Luke 11.11–13).

Questions, doubts

Can our relationship with God survive difficulties? Ancient Hebrew wisdom says that God has set eternity in the core of human beings. But sometimes things happen which cause us to lose sight of that and wonder if he was ever there at all.

People's relationship with God often begins and may continue with questions, as Alex Mowbray wrote in the poem below.

When questions come

Things aren't what they seem
like our slow-rolling world so natural, serene
as seen from out in space;
like those we've known for many years
revealing who they really are;
like what we know of God.
There seems to be a time in everybody's life
when questions come
and answers don't,
when what we think we know is not enough to satisfy
and questioning begins
propelled by sickness or the death of someone near,
relentless reasoning, deep disillusion or a curiosity –
we must know why we're here.
Strangely
the one who only spoke the truth was brutalized;
the perfect man who understood our deepest needs
was left to hang . . .
but you can't kill God for long.

Do people who have been Christians for a while ever have doubts? Well, yes! As with any close human relationship, one with God can go through some rocky times. There may even be separations. Here Sandra Delemare, from the New Forest, writes of her on–off relationship with God.

During my early teens I became an atheist. Studying science, everything seemed cut and dried, with no room for God. Then, in the sixth form, the first thing we learnt was 'deviations from the gas laws' – no real gas obeys the gas laws. Rethinking my philosophy, I became an agnostic.

At university I met some Christians. They didn't answer all my questions, but did convince me that the evidence for Jesus rising from the dead is pretty overwhelming. Also, I found the bond between the Christians attractive. I knew I wasn't 'one of them' and yet I didn't feel excluded. After some months I decided to trust Jesus with my whole self rather than simply believe with my mind. All was well for about six months until I became embroiled in a series of unhelpful relationships. Sometimes, though, I'd be back in church again.

By my mid-twenties I'd thrown in the towel. I had a daughter, without being married, then left her father. She lived with my parents while I did teacher training. After five terms teaching I was advised to give it a rest as I couldn't control the classes. As plans to make a home for the two of us seemed further away than ever I thought that I'd blown it and there was no way out, let alone back to God. I became very depressed, even suicidal at times.

Later I married a man who wasn't a Christian. By my mid-thirties we decided our family was complete and I had a sterilization. When I fell pregnant again my husband was really angry. That's when I prayed, 'Help! If he doesn't want this baby, I can't cope.' Then, a few days after the birth, I had a wonderful experience of knowing God's love and acceptance. He showed me that was what I needed – human love would never satisfy me.

At that point I wanted to start meeting with other Christians again. God seemed to say, 'You look after your baby and family and I will find you a church.' I felt myself drawn to one and the minute I walked through the door I felt at home. Everyone was friendly, seemed interested in me – I recognized the same love that I'd experienced with the Christians at university.

After the dark years of suicidal depressions and one muddle after another, my life took off again. I became a local councillor and a part-time community education worker. I developed my writing – producing a weekly newsletter for the church and letters and articles for the local press.

Things were jogging along nicely until my husband had a psychotic episode, a spending spree and then lost his job. It seemed that we might lose the house, and I feared losing my mind too. It ended up with my going back to university to do a nursing course. Now I work as a mental health nurse and really enjoy it.

All these experiences have taught me to trust God. I had nowhere else to turn, and though the church leadership lent moral support, they could do little practically. These words from the Bible sum up the situation: 'I cried out, "I'm slipping!" and your unfailing love, O Lord, supported me. When doubts filled my mind, your comfort gave me renewed hope and cheer' (Psalm 94.18–19, NLT). In my notebook are many such Bible verses that the Lord highlighted for me at that time. They helped me to keep close to him and to trust him that we would get through.

I often ask myself, 'Why did he intervene then?' I hadn't been to church regularly, read my Bible or prayed properly for years. Why should God bother with me?

Answer: because that's just the way he is. He is love, he is merciful. He never gives up on us. He will always give us another chance. It's never too late. We can really mess up and still be forgiven and change. He's never more than a prayer away. Best of all, I know that nothing can separate me from God's love.

We can run a long way from God. We may doubt him but he doesn't doubt us. Even knowing the worst there is to be known about us, he goes on loving us – as this ancient song from the Bible says:

> Where can I go from your Spirit? Where can I flee from your presence? If I go up to the heavens, you are there; if I make my bed in the depths, you are there. If I rise on the wings of the dawn, if I settle on the far side of the sea, even there your hand will guide me, your right hand will hold me fast. If I say, 'Surely the darkness will hide me and the light become night around me,' even the darkness will not be dark to you; the night will shine like the day, for darkness is as light to you. For you created my inmost being; you knit me together in my mother's womb. I praise you because I am fearfully and wonderfully made; your works are wonderful, I know that full well. My frame was not hidden from you when I was made in the secret place. When I was woven together in the depths of the earth, your eyes saw my unformed body. All the days ordained for me were written in your book before one of them came to be.
>
> (Psalm 139.7–16)

For real, in good times and bad?

Bea Fishback writes:

> Life for my husband and me was like enjoying the perfect wave for surfing, riding the sea of life with enthusiasm and vigour – even if we'd grown a bit 'watery around the knees' from age. Our grown children were in good places in their lives. We had a lovely home, pretty things, purpose in our shared work and we looked forward to the future with excitement. Until two years ago. First my husband was diagnosed with cancer. After two surgeries and a diagnosis of secondary cancer we felt as if we'd fallen off the surfboard and were swimming in the ocean, paddling like mad, with our heads just above water.

Then another crashing wave swept over us. One night, as I prepared for bed, I felt a lump. After consultation and surgery, I too was diagnosed with cancer. At this point we knew we had two choices. We could either rely on God as our life preserver or drown in self-pity. God had always been a part of our lives when everything was good. Would we still look to him when times were bad?

This dilemma would put our faith to the test in ways we never imagined. When we found fears, anxieties and uncertainties overwhelming us, we wondered if our faith would carry us through. But we can say in all honesty that God showed himself faithful in many ways: through the care of family and friends, through our reading the Bible, through a gentle touch or loving embrace, God's love became more real to us than ever before. Cancer is a frightening disease to many people, but we can tell you from experience that God can be relied on to carry us through anything life has to offer – no matter how bad the storm or high the waves.

St Paul had experienced misunderstandings, shipwrecks, beatings, long hot journeys, separations from those he loved, trusted friends who let him down . . . He too spoke from personal experience when he wrote these words in a letter from a prison at the very centre of the mighty Roman Empire, where a death sentence awaited him. That empire fell long ago, yet we can still draw strength from the truth of Paul's words today.

> Who shall separate us from the love of Christ? Shall trouble or hardship or persecution or famine or nakedness or danger or sword? As it is written: 'For your sake we face death all day long; we are considered as sheep to be slaughtered.' No, in all these things we are more than conquerors through him who loved us. For I am convinced that neither death nor life, neither angels nor demons, neither the present nor the future, nor any powers, neither height nor depth, nor anything else in all creation, will

be able to separate us from the love of God that is in Christ Jesus our Lord. (Romans 8.35–39)

Real, even in the depths?

Out of the depths I cry to you, O Lord ... hear my voice. Let your ears be attentive to my cry for mercy ... I wait for the Lord, my soul waits, and in his word I put my hope. My soul waits for the Lord more than watchmen wait for the morning ... O Israel, put your hope in the Lord, for with the Lord is unfailing love and with him is full redemption.

(Psalm 130.1–7)

Psalms are the part of the Bible which formed the worship songbook of ancient Israel. They can differ from songs sung in most churches, in their degree of honesty. The ancient song-writers felt free to tell God when they had reached the depths, to complain that he didn't seem to be listening, that they were having to wait too long for him, even to ask him what he thought he was doing.

Only then something strange happens, nearly always. The dreadful circumstances might not change but somehow the songwriter, in being honest, has reached a place of searingly real communication with God. It's then that he begins to see things in a different way. In Psalm 130 he's waiting in despair – just about clinging on to a little hope in the Lord – and then suddenly, his doubt and gloom gone, he's urging others to put their hope in the Lord's unfailing, redemptive love.

Many Christians will have experienced waiting in a bleak place, with little hope and no sign of God, right when they need him most! It's often only when we look back on such a time that we recognize he never really left us alone. He had been holding us safe in the palm of his loving hand all along.

Hilary Langley was a bright, confident person, a hard worker, good at her job in the Civil Service. Eighty hours a week was nothing unusual – but how long can a person sustain that? After many years she had a nervous breakdown and ended up as an inpatient in a psychiatric hospital, suffering from depression. You can't get much lower than that, or so she thought.

Today she's retired, a happy grandmother who is finding a whole new release in writing. She even wrote her own psalm, expressing some of the questions she still has of God about that time – but seeing his new perspective too.

> Wallowing in the winter of my despair
> Where were you?
> Shackled, ensnared, imprisoned in doubt
> Where were you?
> Cotton wool brain, memory gone, forgotten
> Where were you?
>
> Were you in those sharing my despair?
> With the injured, the homeless, the lost?
> Were you with the druggies, the rapists,
> the murderers, the killers of my soul?
> Were you with the victims, the poor, the bereaved?
> Did they know you were there?
> How did they know?
>
> Were you the light at the end of the endless tunnel,
> the hint of music in the air beyond the prison cell?
> Were you in the smiles, the caring, the love
> of those with, and alongside, me?
> Were you in the pain of my renewing emotion,
> the agony of my recall, the tenuous hope of recovery?
>
> When it is most dark you are there.
> Light comes from the dark and
> winter gives rise to spring.
> We may not hear you, cannot see you

but you are at our side.
You take on our pain, nudging us
into spring.
You are the purity of birdsong,
the colour of the flowers,
the warmth of the sun
and the promise of life begun anew.

You might like to consider these words of St Paul:

Now we see but a poor reflection as in a mirror; then we shall
see face to face. Now I know in part; then I shall know fully,
even as I am fully known.   (1 Corinthians 13.12)

For real, now?

Elisabeth from west Wales writes of an ongoing illness which
had a profound effect on her family:

Bipolar depression, like a pendulum, sets the whole of family
and social life on a see-saw, swinging it, at times, out of human
control.

My husband, an able and creative lecturer and language
teacher, was well known and respected. His mood swings showed
up first in the middle years of our married life when our three
children were of primary school age.

Previously a contented and joyous man with no signs of
depression, he returned from a teaching weekend saying, 'I'm
ill.' For the following months he seemed a timid shadow of himself, completely dependent on all of us – especially me.

Through the next 12 years of his life, the 'lows' were infrequent
and the 'highs' almost constant – bordering at times on danger-
ously high. Under a cloudless sky, his hyperactivity lifted him
to a mood of celestial well-being.

A visiting preacher was in the pulpit and visitors in the congregation at our chapel one Sunday morning in August when

my husband was giving the week's announcements. He did that often. Only this time his delivery became a peroration.

Another deacon's attempts to control his flow of words failed. Listening, I prayed fervently. Then, feeling completely helpless, slowly I got up out of my pew, walked right to the front and stood beside him.

Almost immediately, I believe, he acknowledged God's presence and sat down gently. I then proceeded to pick up the offering plate and walked from pew to pew, receiving money gifts for the church while the organ played.

I'm sure that God answered my prayer then. It was a different story one weekday afternoon. Being a gifted communicator, my husband was often invited to address public meetings. This particular engagement entailed driving 45 miles south, via his home village, to a remote chapel.

He was 'high' – insistent on going, on driving himself and picking up his bachelor brother en route. I knew I had to accompany him and was very apprehensive, praying anxiously, begging God to intervene. When that prayer wasn't answered it created a barrier of disappointment and mistrust between me and God. I felt bruised and wounded.

So is God real? Is he always in control? Today, 20 years on, I say that he is. There's mystery. I don't understand why he intervenes sometimes and doesn't at others. My husband was not healed of his bipolar depression before he died. Yet by God's grace I know that I'm being restored and healed. I am becoming an overcomer.

Jesus, when he walked this earth, healed a lot of people and told his followers to heal the sick in his name. Some are healed when Christians pray today. Many more are not. We might wonder, therefore, if Jesus and his promises are for real. Especially if our prayers for a sick loved one go unanswered or if the illness affects the mind, changing, at the most fundamental level, the person we once knew.

Psalm 142 (below) is just as honest as Psalm 130 and Hilary's own psalm. Despite the psalmist's faith, God doesn't appear to take action to help. As with Elisabeth's story, the reasons why he doesn't always rush in to rescue or heal never become clear. And yet, though desperate, none of these people have lost their faith – their ultimate trust in their Lord – nor lost sight of the fact that he does care, does love them and will restore hope. They know this person is who he says he is – because they know *him*.

I cry aloud to the LORD; I lift up my voice to the LORD for mercy. I pour out my complaint before him; before him I tell my trouble. When my spirit grows faint within me, it is you who know my way. In the path where I walk men have hidden a snare for me. Look to my right and see; no-one is concerned for me. I have no refuge; no-one cares for my life. I cry to you, O LORD; I say, 'You are my refuge, my portion in the land of the living.' Listen to my cry, for I am in desperate need; rescue me from those who pursue me, for they are too strong for me. Set me free from my prison, that I may praise your name. Then the righteous will gather about me because of your goodness to me. (Psalm 142)

Outworking

'Too heavenly minded to be of any earthly use' – I've met a few like that; they appear to be living on another planet or in some ethereal dimension. Loving feelings aren't much use if they have no practical outworking. On the other hand, people whose faith helps and inspires them to make a difference now, here, on this planet, convince me of the reality of their relationship with God. They are doing what Jesus did – and his love wasn't ethereal.

Real empowering

'I do like working with Annemarie,' said a friend. 'Helping people with multiple needs and complex disabilities can be so challenging – for example, when you're supervising lunchtime and one person's behaviour affects others. When I asked Annemarie why it's always calm when she's on lunchtime duty with me she said, "Perhaps because I'm praying."'

I had been thinking about how people's relationship with God can make a difference in difficult situations, so asked my friend if I could meet with her colleague, Annemarie Aurmoogum. Now in her sixties, Annemarie told me how she'd come to England from Mauritius at 19 and trained as a nurse. Growing up a Roman Catholic, she'd always believed in God but he wasn't the focus of her life until, during her husband's last illness, she started questioning what life was all about. A friend took her to another church on a day when the preacher spoke from Galatians 5: 'The fruit of the Spirit is love, joy, peace, patience, kindness, goodness, faithfulness, gentleness and self-control . . . Since we live by the Spirit, let us keep in step with the Spirit' (Galatians 5.22–23, 25).

Here am I, she thought, at the end of my tether with constant work and worry – my husband's terminal illness, an uncertain future, supporting our daughters at university . . . can the Holy Spirit really bear the weight of all that? And if he gave me those good 'fruits' might I be able to help others better? She told me:

> That's what happened. I no longer worry. My husband died five years ago but I know what life's about now – loving God and loving people. I've so much purpose and direction. People say that I bring peace into situations, though my love's not as selfless as Jesus' is. My work is still hard and I never know what might happen on a shift – but now I trust God will help and give me patience, gentleness and all the rest of that good 'fruit'.
>
> As I talk with him throughout the day he helps me see how to pray for people and build up relationships of trust, even with the most volatile ones. We're given good training in the workplace but in addition God inspires me as to how I can communicate positively. He has taught me his language of love, which doesn't rely on words. One woman is blind and deaf, with severe learning difficulties, but when I touch her arm she knows it's me and becomes happy instead of frustrated.
>
> If other staff are less than patient and kind, I pray for them quietly. Often the Holy Spirit shows me what lies behind their attitude. He gives me something positive to say or do for them. You know, harsh words can reduce a person to nothing, while God-inspired words can bring her right up again. The Holy Spirit is gentle; he listens – and through us he can bring light to people in the most difficult situations.

No matter how hard we try, we can't do things on our own – but God never intended us to live without his help. In particular, he sent the Holy Spirit to stay closer to us than our own heart-beat. His fruit takes time to grow in people's lives, but before too long the difference can be remarkable – Annemarie had found the reality of God at work in her life only eight years before our conversation. As well as Galatians 5's words about the fruits of the Holy Spirit, the following passages may help show how the Holy Spirit can be real in our lives, helping us every day to live out his loving plan. We may not understand, nor receive all of his gifts and fruit at once, but the Holy Spirit will always give us the far greater gift of himself.

> Unless I go away, the Counsellor will not come to you; but if I go, I will send him to you . . . when he, the Spirit of truth, comes, he will guide you into all truth.　　　　　(John 16.7, 13)

> To each one the manifestation of the Spirit is given for the common good. To one there is given through the Spirit the message of wisdom, to another the message of knowledge by means of the same Spirit, to another faith by the same Spirit, to another gifts of healing by that one Spirit, to another miraculous powers, to another prophecy . . .　　　(1 Corinthians 12.7–10)

Real principles that work

Don't be misled: No one makes a fool of God. What a person plants, he will harvest. The person who plants selfishness, ignoring the needs of others – ignoring God! – harvests a crop of weeds. All he'll have to show for his life is weeds! But the one who plants in response to God, letting God's Spirit do the growth work in him, harvests a crop of real life, eternal life.

So let's not allow ourselves to get fatigued doing good. At the right time we will harvest a good crop if we don't give up, or quit. Right now, therefore, every time we get the chance, let us work for the benefit of all, starting with the people closest to us in the community of faith.　　(Galatians 6.7–10, *The Message*)

If our relationship with God is real and changes us, we'd expect it to affect all areas of our life, including our fellow Christians, our friends, family, work . . . How can we make things better for other people? How would God do that?

What is this 'crop of real, eternal life'? Part of it concerns his ways which, if applied to our society, would make things better for a lot of people. For example – rest. One of the ten commandments tells us to rest one day a week. Two reasons are given. One is because God rested after he made the earth. He's not 'driven', as so many of us are these days. He 'sits back' sometimes and enjoys what he's made, pronouncing it 'good'.

The second reason is that the people he was then working with, Israel, knew what it was to be slaves in Egypt. Their history taught them how terrible that had been, so now they should consider those working for them – treat them as human beings, allowing them rest sometimes. Sadly, some Christianized societies have interpreted this commandment by imposing a rigid and sombre 'Sunday', but God knows we all need times to play, relax, enjoy ourselves and one another, as well as times to work – and to enjoy worshipping him.

As we learn God's ways we find they are not restrictive but good for us – all of us, as we interact. Maybe this is part of what Jesus meant when he prayed, 'Father, your kingdom (your rule, your way of doing things) come on earth as it is in heaven.'

Paul Lambert is an organizational consultant within a small company which looks at 'whole systems' – for example, a large enterprise, or care for the elderly by all agencies across an English county. The six core members of that company, including Paul, are Christians who base their business ethics and advice on principles they've learnt from knowing God for themselves – and reading in the Bible about the way he treats groups and organizations.

So, for example, they will run an initial workshop with the top people within a large firm, asking what they think is its purpose. 'To make money,' the MD of a railway company might say. The head of engineering has a different perspective, 'It's to implement everything we need to make these railways run.'

The conversation changes attitudes by getting everyone thinking about and eventually agreeing upon what they are striving to be and to do as an enterprise. Paul told me:

> Being – identity and purpose – comes before doing. First of all, and at the centre of himself and of everything, God is. Then, out of the central 'being' of God you can see the three persons of the Trinity having integrated functions. The Father is strategic, the Son embodies those strategies (systems) and the Holy Spirit sees to their completion and evaluation.

Seeking to understand God's person and ways can lead to a real practical understanding of the complex work of large organizations. For example, a multinational railway company had become dysfunctional because each team lacked control within itself of what it was doing. This meant individuals were suffering stress of lifespan-reducing proportions. Once all were integrated into a community in which each team could take control and responsibility for their own particular area, each served the whole better. When individuals' talents were used more effectively, stress reduced.

Another example concerned care for the elderly within a county – failing because each organization did its own thing. Representatives of over 100 of these organizations came together in a workshop to look at the problems. If transport, hospitals, GPs, home support, occupational therapy, social services, hospices, care homes, carers and all the rest saw themselves as parts of an integrated whole, with each aware of what everyone else could offer, they would greatly enhance the quality of life (and death) for a large population of elderly people. That was their core purpose. In addition, money wouldn't be wasted, for example keeping individuals in acute hospital beds when they would be far happier with appropriate care elsewhere.

Paul told me about an organization with 86,000 employees that asked his firm to arrange training for their up-and-coming senior leaders. Most would have chosen the brightest and best and sent them on a residential course in a country house. Paul said, 'If you want not high-fliers but people who engage with clients' benefit and welfare, then they need experience-based training.' He arranged this with an organization which placed those trainee leaders to help front-line charities such as those offering drug rehabilitation. They faced very real challenges there but, rather than 'bossing', developed an attitude of service and achieved a real understanding of people and of the difficulties some faced.

You might ask God about how these Bible verses could be applied in your life and work and among all the people you meet, day by day: 'Each of you should look not only to your own interests, but also to the interests of others' (Philippians 2.4).

> Speaking the truth in love, we will in all things grow up into him who is the Head, that is, Christ. From him the whole body, joined and held together by every supporting ligament, grows and builds itself up in love, as each part does its work.
>
> (Ephesians 4.15–16)

Real abroad – and at work

Christians are all individuals but there are real family resemblances. We share, give or take a few minor details, similar values and morality. We might annoy each other but most Christians, most of the time, are loving, kind, welcoming and full of grace. We love, trust and worship the same God. So in order to learn and grow in our relationship with God, wouldn't it be best to mix only with other Christians?

Some churches would agree, yet this seemingly safe option is not one Jesus told his followers to take. Instead, according to Matthew's Gospel, his last words to them involved a lot of risk – unless they really did trust him. In those days, the Roman Empire believed that it had final authority on earth – and executed those who disagreed. But Jesus said:

> 'All authority in heaven and on earth has been given to me. Therefore go and make disciples of all nations, baptising them in the name of the Father and of the Son and of the Holy Spirit, and teaching them to obey everything I have commanded you. And surely I am with you always, to the very end of the age.'
>
> (Matthew 28.18–20)

The question is, where is the Lord and where does he hold sway? Not just in church! Psalm 24.1 says: 'The earth is the LORD's, and everything in it, the world, and all who live in it.' If the whole earth is his, if his authority extends to all of heaven and earth, then I can relate to him everywhere, even if I'm the only person for miles around who acknowledges his presence and authority. I needn't be on the defensive. He's with me; he will help me to make his presence, ways and authority known.

I heard a talk by a young man who is both a Christian and a tabloid journalist. This, he explained, need not be a contradiction in terms. Standing up for what he believes isn't easy – but not impossible. He's never been forced to compromise. Instead, his faith can work for him. People often trust him instinctively, opening up to him rather than to other journalists. He doesn't betray their trust, continues to care for them over the months and then finds the conversation may turn to God, who can bring comfort to distraught families. That journalist is often the only Christian presence within tragic situations – thank God for him! It happens because he trusts God enough to take risks and he gave many instances of knowing God's protection when his work took him, undercover, into highly dangerous situations.

John Ripley is another person whose relationship with God has taken him out of 'safe' areas. I used to pray regularly with his wife who often mentioned that John was in some far-flung corner of the earth on behalf of the multinational company where he held a senior management position. But aren't these multinationals today's all-powerful baddies, exploiting the developing world? And didn't John share God's passion for the world's poor and marginalized, as well as heading up the team which looked after our church's missionaries? After a while I asked John how he reconciled this with his employment.

John said they didn't have to conflict. Good management practice and committed employers could arrange for improvements to such things as housing, water supply and education within a poor community – which would enable its people either to start working, or to work more efficiently, for the company. He's a man of prayer and God-given vision. God would help him see how to work things out in this win–win fashion. I smiled too at the way John would 'piggy-back' onto his work trips visits to encourage missionary contacts of our church, from Brazil to Siberia! I asked him to explain some more how all this came about. He writes:

> At university I was heading for my long-term plan – scientific research – when I began to doubt the level of dedication to theory and equations that this might entail. One particular role model, a tutor who subsequently won his Nobel Prize, was quite convincing, without intending to be – I was not enamoured with the rest of his life.

So I explored management traineeships alongside research options and ended up with various offers in science and one management scheme. Should I change direction? I set aside an afternoon of intensive prayer. It was as if God was saying that he would go with me – if I took a risk.

I pursued this option and had an extremely unusual offer letter, containing the phrase, 'If you are prepared to take the risk of joining us, we are prepared to take you.' Some 35 years later, I retired as one of the most senior members of the multinational – and both sides would say the risks we took have brought reward!

My career showed me a lot of the world. I spent much time in developing countries. I am convinced that enterprise fulfils a creation principle and that economic development does more than anything (even aid) to relieve poverty. Nevertheless, the question would occur from time to time – is there a more direct contribution you can and should make? I read something of Cliff Richard's reaction when first seeing poverty with the Christian charity Tearfund – should he do more directly? But it was as if God passed on to me the same answer – 'You do what you do best,' in my case business leadership, 'and use that to address the issues.'

Still, work practices aren't always a good fit with God's values – on how we spend our time, for example. Accountants are always under pressure at year ends; it takes the shine off Christmas and the New Year! I took over a leading role in a subsidiary at a time when the accounts had to be finished by the third Thursday. The previous year, that had given 17 days – and the team had worked every single one of them, New Year's Day and Sundays included.

Convinced of the importance of family time and that we are not designed for continuous working, I announced that we would not work on the bank holiday or Sundays, taking our available days from 17 last year down to 13 this year. People's energy kept up so well that we finished on day ten, leaving the luxury of three days to check everything and produce an even higher standard of accounts. It's easy, in hindsight, to see why that happened, but it takes courage to change things and put God's ways into practice.

It was never easy to know how overt to be as a Christian in a multi-ethnic, multicultural, multinational company. I guess my approach found some echoes of St Francis: 'Preach the gospel always; if necessary, use words.' There are some times to speak, but always ones to listen, care and engage.

I did not appreciate how much my colleagues knew that faith was a key factor for me – until tragedy struck. We lost our 21-year-old second daughter in very difficult circumstances. Now that is a challenge – to keep believing, going to church, achieving in life . . . But this is how my colleagues reacted. Many wrote with phrases like, 'We are glad you have a faith to carry you through,' or, 'I don't know how anyone could handle this without a God.' Over 60 colleagues of many backgrounds – faiths and no faith – came to the memorial service. Some continued to share their tragedies and challenges. Looking back, this horrible period was a key to even more open relationships.

Lord, I see the reality of the outworking of people's relationship with you more clearly outside of holy huddles than in church. Thank you for all those who trust you enough to stick to your ways, to acknowledge your authority and risk following your instructions in situations that seem unlikely. Help us to do the same!

Real compassion

Jesus said: 'A man was going down from Jerusalem to Jericho, when he fell into the hands of robbers. They stripped him of his clothes, beat him and went away, leaving him half-dead. A priest happened to be going down the same road, and when he saw the man, he passed by on the other side. So too, a Levite . . . But a Samaritan, as he travelled, came where the man was; and when he saw him, he took pity on him. He went to him and bandaged his wounds, pouring on oil and wine. Then he put the man on his own donkey, brought him to an inn and took care of him. (Luke 10.30–34)

God's relationship with us isn't meant to turn us all pious. Jesus said there are only two things we need to do: love God with all our heart and mind and soul and strength and love our neighbour as we do ourselves. When asked, 'Who is my neighbour?' he told this story in which religious leaders wouldn't risk stopping to help an injured crime victim. With important sacred duties to perform, best stay clean and pretend they hadn't noticed! Eventually, a man whose religious affiliation was considered suspect rescued the man. We know him as 'the Good Samaritan'. Normally Jews and Samaritans would have despised and avoided one another – but in this man compassion won out over religious barriers, pleasing God.

However much we pray, go to church, read the Bible and so on, a failure to show compassion towards fellow human beings will damage our relationship with God, who loves others as well as ourselves. It hurts him if we turn our backs on them. And we'd be going against his most cherished values. God is full of compassion. Religion doesn't cut it: love does.

Hilary Allen, a GP in Somerset, writes:

It's God's fault! He opened my eyes to the needs of people in my town centre late at night. For years I'd driven around in the small hours, when on duty as a GP, observing their plight – the vulnerability of the scantily clad young girls, the aggressive drunken behaviour of men, the ensuing fights and tears, the vomit and debris on the pavements. I felt sad – was this what was meant by 'having a good time'? I suppose that was how God began to plant within me seeds of a deep concern for these marginalized people who were at such a distance from knowing God or relating to him in any way.

Now I've trained as a Street Pastor and volunteer as part of a team, being there for them on a Saturday night. Late on during my first duty, a fight broke out among nightclub revellers. Casualties groaned, awaiting an ambulance. As I knelt alongside one of the guys, assessing his condition, I was fully aware of many eyes boring into the back of my jacket which was emblazoned 'Street Pastor'. I couldn't hide why I was there and could hear their praise, but then thought to myself: Hilary, how often are you kneeling in the gutter at 3.30 in the morning, taking risks like this? Instantly, I felt so peaceful. I knew that if Jesus was walking the town today, this is exactly what he'd be doing. But he isn't here on earth in bodily form any more. Instead, Christians act as his hands and feet. If I love him, of course I should be doing what he would do.

Street Pastors work from a position of compassion and love, relating to people in practical ways. We're out in all weathers, unpaid, late at night, simply showing that we care – and it gets to people, they can't explain it away! The reality is I'd rather be snug in my slumbers, especially when the temperature is sub-zero but I know that God showed me this path of service. I can't manufacture the different qualities and skills needed but I've seen him graciously equip and enable me to share his love with others. This relationship with him is real, all right! I know I'm inadequate, having nothing in common with the party-goers, yet God uses Street Pastors and touches all we meet. I'm privileged to be part of this amazing work and feel closer than ever to God when I know that he is helping me to help others in such difficult situations.

I talked with Fran Pyatt during her first week of maternity leave from her work with the Christian relief and development agency Tearfund. She told me:

I was with Tearfund in Liberia when I realized I was pregnant, at the time of the massive earthquake in Haiti. A friend phoned me from all the chaos there, saying they needed me, a French-speaker.

I longed to go but knew I couldn't camp out, work 16-hour days and risk dodgy food and water while expecting a baby. I'd only have got in the way. So, here I am, back in the middle-class village where I spent my teens, when right now Tearfund are involved with the devastating floods in Pakistan ...

I was based there at our HQ in Islamabad for five weeks, giving cover over Christmas and the New Year following an earthquake in the mountains in October 2005. Before I arrived, the UN had allocated each of the relief agencies particular communities to supply with equipment to build shelters. My job was to chase up the goods we had ordered and to organize their transport before winter snows blocked the mountain roads.

What difference does it make, being a Christian, working for a Christian organization? All the agencies do a good job, so that's not a simple question to answer. I started work in logistics for a commercial firm. Relief work's not so different – you get on with the job as professionally as possible, fit into the team, try to adapt to cultural differences. But working all hours, every day, people tend to start 'running on empty', so it helps when the team support each other in prayer. We prayed too for the snows to be delayed – and they were. Snow belted down just 24 hours after we'd delivered everything.

We employed a number of Pakistanis whose Christian faith meant they had seldom been given work before they came to us. They were so thankful and worked incredibly hard. I learnt a lot from them. In the mountains an excellent team of Muslim men distributed our supplies, led by one young Christian woman from Scotland. They were really good to her. Sometimes we'd find Islam's fatalism hindering relief work but these guys challenged her own faith because of their strong commitment and compassionate motivation.

Not everyone supplying aid is good, however. One firm drenched tents in water – the more they weighed, the more they could charge for their transport. A wealthy Arab showed us superb toolkits for erecting temporary shelters. When they arrived, late, the quality was terrible. I said we wouldn't pay the full price for them but he didn't care, he'd made so much money already out of the earthquake. I had to remain polite, logical and firm when people told lies, broke promises or profiteered from the suffering of others.

Not everyone is compassionate, nor is compassion exclusive to Christians – but we have pioneered in some areas and others have followed. For example, in Tearfund we try to be accountable not only to donors but to the people we serve, giving them a chance to voice complaints and suggestions.

I'm looking forward to this baby being born in a week or two but I'm going to miss being out in the field, doing what I can.

Compassion fatigue sets in very easily where the problems seem too large or too many; too far away or too threateningly near. One person can't solve all the world's woes but we can all do something, especially with God's help.

Last word

———•◆•———

Is God for real? Let's turn the question around and ask it from God's point of view. Am I for real? Are you? He believes that we are. He thinks we're worth knowing, worth dying for. I find that truly astounding.

So, applying the same shift in perspective, don't read the Bible – let it read you. Believe in heaven and you'll see it. What seems so solidly real through our human eyes for our brief time on this earth is only a tiny fragment of the reality that's 'out there'. Stretching further than the telescope can see and coming closer than the microscope can focus is God – bringing life, eternal life. Real – oh yes! Not reality as we know it, though – far, far better!